M.a.r.r.i.a.g.e:
God's Way

DR. ARVIL JONES

Copyright 2017
By Dr. Arvil Jones
ISBN 978-1-940609-85-0 Soft cover

All rights reserved. No part of this book may be reproduced or transmitted in any form or by any means, electronic or mechanical, including photocopying, recording, or by any information storage and retrieval system, without permission in writing from the copyright owner.
This book was printed in the United States of America.

To order additional copies of this book contact:
Dr. Arvil Jones
Cjones156@cinci.rr.com
513-907-7751
1304 Bonacker Ave.
Hamilton, Ohio 45011

ACKNOWLEDGEMENT

I want to gratefully acknowledge the invaluable aid of a dear friend of my wife and I, Judy Jordan. Before writing the chapter entitled – The "rr" in Marriage = Railroad, I consulted Judy, asking for her expertise, which she graciously offered. Judy retired from the Railroad,  having served, first as a brakeman, then as a conductor, an engineer, and finally rose to the position of Yard Master. Her knowledge of how a railroad operates has helped me tremendously in drawing comparisons between a railroad and a Marriage.

FOREWORD

Marriage is a commitment to spend the rest of your life with one person. It doesn't come with details of everything you will go through, and no two days are ever the same. Dr. Jones has, in his inimitable manner, written the true meaning of marriage, and what God intended it to be, using the Bible, God's Word, as well as his own marriage to his beautiful wife Carolyn Jones as his guide to write this wonderful book.

This book will lead you and guide you through the steps of marriage while using God's love to show you the way. You can have a good marriage even through the rough times that are bound to come. It will help and prepare you for what to expect once you make those vows before saying - "I do". God wants you to have a loving, happy marriage. Dr. Arvil Jones shows you how to do that through the things he has written and learned through his own experiences, as a Pastor, teacher, and counselor.

No matter where you are in your marriage, or if you are preparing to take your vows with the one you love, this book will help you. After reading it you will be so happy you did. This little book can help you avoid so many obstacles and errors that can either make or break your life with the one who means so much to you. Marriage is a commitment for the rest of your life, and it can be either the worst, or the best decision you ever made.

God bless you on this wonderful journey!

---Eva Dimel

INTRODUCTION

Someday my children, my grandchildren, and my great grandchildren will read this little book, and it is not likely that I will be here when the great grandchildren read it. And if that should be the case, I want them to know the heart and character of their ancestor, and at least be pleased with him, even if they cannot be proud of him. I was asked by a fellow minister to write this book, and although it has been one of the most difficult and thought-provoking books I have written to date, it has also been one of the greatest joys of my life. You, the reader, depending upon your own personal relationship to Christ, and your personal views on certain modern issues, may find some, or all of this book offensive, or even in poor taste. And if that should be the case, please know that the author did not intend to offend anyone. But please know also that the author will never apologize for anything he has written in these pages. It may be that some of my friends will someday read this book, and if they do, I pray that if their opinion of me is no better than before reading this book, hopefully it will be no worse.

I come from a different time than many of my younger acquaintances - a time when the mentality of the younger folks seemed to be at war with the mentality of my generation. That war has escalated in intensity to the present day. But since I have more days behind me than I have in front of me, this old soldier chooses to stick to his guns, offering no compromise for his convictions, though he be shelled with every newfangled weaponry his adversaries may invent. I, and a few others, are at war with every man woman and child who would cast aspersions upon the sanctity and sacredness of that blessed institution we call Marriage. With every ounce of strength in every sinew of my aging body, I vow to defend to the death the sanctity of that most blessed and sacred of all human relationships. If ever a soldier has believed in the righteousness of the cause for which he is willing to lay down his life, let me borrow from the revered Martin Luther, and say – here I stand, I can do no other. It would be no less than treason against my King and His kingdom for me to stand idly by and say or do nothing while the adversaries of truth continuously bombard His castle. And if these feeble fingers should fail to write all that needs to be written, may God grant that someone else might take up my fallen sword, and run into the battle in my place, unafraid and unashamed to carry on a fight that must be won at all cost, lest our descendants be ashamed of us in the end. The golden shield of Marriage has been dented and tarnished by her enemies – Oh God of Heaven, let me be the one who restores her to her former glory, even if it costs my life.

Contents

The "M" in Marriage = Mistakes! 11

The "M" in Marriage = Mistakes! continued 43

The "a" in Marriage = Authority 61

The "rr" in Marriage = Railroad 75

The "i" in Marriage = Intimacy 87

The "a" in Marriage = Alteratives 113

The "g" in Marriage = God 125

The "g" in Marriage = Godless 141

The "e" in Marriage = Endured vs Enduring 145

The "e" in Marriage = Enduring 161

Chapter One

Marriage is honorable in all, and the bed undefiled: but whoremongers and adulterers God will judge (Hebrews 13:4 KJV).

The "M" in Marriage = Mistakes!

Why, you may ask, would any author, and especially a Pastor, begin a study on such a profound and sacred subject as Marriage with the very first chapter being entitled – Mistakes? The answer, my answer, may be as profound as the subject itself. If statistics prove anything (sometimes they do not,) then there are millions of reasons for beginning this book this way, because there are literally millions of marriages which, if defined and described with total honesty, would have to be characterized as colossal mistakes. Please note here that I have not yet begun to list or enumerate the many mistakes that occur in marriages *after* the ceremony, the honeymoon, and the children. I am simply stating without reservation that millions of marriages were *mistakes* at the beginning – they should never have happened! And in my humble opinion, this is becoming more and more the rule rather than the exception with the passing of time.

For the purpose of this little book, I did not consult any other outside source. I did not consult a library (personal or public,) and neither have I turned to any of the countless works of other men and women on the subject. I will be the first to acknowledge that you, the reader, can probably find, or have already found, several books, written by far greater authors than myself on the subject of Marriage. I do not claim any degree of expertise, and neither am I any kind of authority on the subject. When it was suggested that I write this book, I had to chuckle just a bit, wondering why anyone would ask me to write a book on such a sacred subject as Marriage, seeing I have only been married to the same woman for forty-nine years. Some of you may think forty-nine years of marriage should make me a bit of an authority on the subject, but I must immediately confess that I am still a student, and not an authority, and definitely not an expert.

You may find, however, that this little work is somewhat different from most others you have read on this blessed subject. Most of the books I have read on Marriage tend to tell us how to make our marriages better, how to improve our relationship with our spouse and/or children, how to avoid certain mistakes (major and minor,) and how to recognize certain trends or habits that may be adversely affecting our marriages in one way or another. And there are a few books out there which, if read and followed, could have some positive and lasting effects upon marriages that have gotten into trouble for some reason. And I have heard many testimonies to the positive effects many couples have experienced as the result of either reading the powerful and profound works of notable ministers and counselors, or having gone to counseling sessions with a well-trained marriage counselor.

    If this book is to be worth the price you paid for it, and if it does indeed make a difference in your life, it will not be because it is simply in a different format, or from a different author - it will be because the author has been on his knees before God in fervent prayer for guidance in the writing of it. If this book is to make any difference at all, it will be because it sprang from a righteous motive, with the intent to glorify God, and to help my fellow man. This book is being written in the hope that you, the reader, when, or even before you are finished with this book, will quickly lay it aside, and run to your Bible for the help you need. Dear reader, I beg of you, beware the man or woman who lays claim to any degree of divine inspiration in his or her written works. There is one, and only one, inspired Book – The Holy

Bible. Neither this book, nor any other is inspired, as the Bible is inspired. And yet the author feels compelled to write it. Let the reader discern and judge the motive behind the writing of it.

    I am doubtful that I will even deal with many (if any) of the mistakes that occur in marriages *after the ceremony* has taken place. As I have said, there are countless other well-written books on the market today which deal with many of those mistakes. Unless this writer feels compelled at some point to deal with a few of those mistakes, he will confine his comments to the mistakes that are made *before the marriage ceremony*.

    How many modern marriages were destined to fail before the ceremony took place - only God knows for sure. In my many years of experience as a Pastor, Evangelist, Author, Teacher and Counselor, I have read many books and listened to many sermons and lectures on the subject of Marriage. I have heard many speakers and writers liken Marriage unto a building, with some referring to a house in which a family is destined to live, and others referring to another type of building or structure. Most of these speakers and writers begin their analogies by asserting that a Marriage, like a building, must first have a solid and secure foundation. And while this assertion is very admirable, and no doubt set forth with the best of intentions, it does not begin at the beginning. In this particular section of this book, I wish to discuss what I believe are five major mistakes that are made prior to most wedding ceremonies, mistakes which are made, not only by the prospective bride and groom themselves, but by others also, including the minister who performs the ceremony.

Before there can be a foundation, there must first be an idea, a thought, a vision in the mind of someone who wants to either build a structure, or have it built by someone else. For the purpose of this study, let's assume we are planning on having a house built – a house in which we are planning on living and raising a family – a house that is destined to be – not just a house, but a home. We want this house to be beautiful, strong, and able to withstand any storm that may beat against it. We want it to last beyond our own lifetime, perhaps to several generations to come. The idea has now become a plan, but so far, it is only our own plan, with no one else involved. If we are wise, we will consult an architect, and not just any architect, but a reputable architect who has vast experience in designing plans for buildings that are able to withstand hurricane-force winds, hail, and all other forces of nature that may come against it. We want the architect to design a plan which includes the foundation and the building itself, from bottom to top. We sit down with the architect. We share our idea with him. We tell him what we have in mind. If the architect is interested in our idea, he will not only listen intently, he will also offer his own ideas, even though they may conflict with our own. If the architect is as good as his reputation declares him to be, he will not only submit a plan with all the dimensions of the foundation and structure, but he will also include a list of all materials necessary to complete the whole project.

Once the architect has "***signed off***", or put his seal and/or signature on the plans – his job is done. It is now up to the builders themselves to properly follow the plans submitted. But let me hesitate right here, and assure you – any architect who is worth his salt will not, after signing off on his plans, immediately abandon the project, and turn to another customer, forgetting all about the plans he just handed to the person who will eventually occupy the house. If he really cares about his own integrity, and the integrity of the house that will eventually spring from his plan, he will follow up on his design, he will stop by and inspect the project while it is yet in the building stage, and he will offer suggestions to the builders themselves, until the last nail is driven. If the builders have faithfully followed the plan from beginning to end, then the structure will be a thing of beauty, reflecting the honor, pride and integrity of the architect and the builders. It will be a structure in which the ones who occupy it will feel proud, safe and comfortable.

But what if the *idea* was all wrong? What if the one who wanted the house built had an ulterior, self-serving motive which included no one but himself? What if, instead of listening to the wise architect, he insists upon his own plans and materials? What if he has no knowledge of how a foundation is to be prepared, and yet insists upon his own design? I trust the reader can see the ramifications of these foolish decisions. A house built by an inexperienced builder with no definitive plans may suffice, and it may even stand for a lifetime, and be suitable to the person occupying it. But that house will ultimately cost the owner far more than he wants to pay. A single nail, either left out or improperly driven can cost the price of a new roof. A foundation that is not properly prepared and perfectly level will result in cracked walls, floors and ceilings. That house could have been far better and far more beautiful and practical had he listened to the wise architect. As the reader can readily see, this analogy could go much farther than the writer has taken it.

I cannot number the counseling sessions in which I have engaged, including marital, pre-marital, child, adolescent, singles and groups of all ages and genders. And the discoveries I have made as a result of those sessions far outnumber the sessions themselves. And I can almost read the thoughts of the reader who is reading this right now – asking if I was able to save any troubled marriages. I must confess; that is a difficult question to answer. In fact, my answer to that question would take up more time and paper than either I or the reader can spare. Let me answer this way: A few of the wedding ceremonies I have performed have resulted in marriages that have lasted a lifetime, while more than a few have ended in disaster, to put it mildly. But if the reader will allow the writer a bit of license, I have always left myself a loophole when performing wedding ceremonies. I never fail to tell the bride and groom that it is not ministers who make marriages!

If ministers could make happy, successful marriages, there would be no need for marriage counselors or divorce lawyers. Yes, I do feel a definite responsibility in performing wedding ceremonies, and I hold myself accountable to some degree if and when any of those marriages *fail*. That is one of the many compelling reasons for this book – my own guilty conscience for having put my signature upon a marriage license, knowing in my heart the marriage was doomed from the beginning! Let me put it another way.

Rather than claim that I may have *saved* a troubled marriage or two; I may have *temporarily prevented* a divorce or two. Not only is it impossible for a minister to *make* a marriage, it is equally impossible for him to *save* it. If a troubled marriage, on the brink of destruction is to be saved, it will be God who saves it. God may use us puny humans as His instrument, but it is He who does the work.

Now, let us go back to the analogy of a marriage and a house. In this imperfect world, there are no perfect men, no perfect ideas, no perfect architects, no perfect materials, no perfect plans, and therefore, no perfect houses – period. And since there are no perfect men, and no perfect women, and no perfect ministers, there are, therefore, no perfect marriages. Sin has blighted everything that now exists. No matter how well-laid or how well-intended, the best plans that men can make are tainted to some degree. But will the reader agree that an idea that begins well, submitted to a highly trained and reputable architect, and fashioned by skilled workmen, stands a far greater chance of producing a beautiful, strong and comfortable house than one that sprang from less than noble motives, and was fashioned by the ignoble hands of the unskilled man himself? But have we not all, at one time or another, seen the most beautiful house that men could build, spoiled, marred, dilapidated and ruined by the occupant? Even with the best architect or architects that money can hire, using the best materials money can buy, and with the most skilled laborers doing the work, many a beautiful home has been marred from without, and destroyed from within.

For a Marriage, there is one, and only one, ***perfect Architect***. His name is Jesus Christ. He has a ***perfect plan*** for Marriage; it is called the Holy Bible. This plan quite often comes into conflict with the best plans that men can produce. And here is where the analogy of a marriage and a house breaks down. If the idea, the notion, the thought, or the full-blown plan for marriage has entered the mind of a man or woman; ***he or she must not submit his or her plan to the Architect, but rather submit to the plan the Architect has already made!*** Will this ensure a happy and successful marriage every time? No, it will not. Not even a perfect Plan, drawn by a perfect Architect, when followed by imperfect men and women, using imperfect materials, can produce a perfect product. But will the reader agree that the marriage built upon the perfect plan of God stands a far better chance of survival and serenity than the marriage that is ***not built*** upon that plan?

Like a house that began as a ***bad idea*** and wound up a disaster, a marriage, improperly imagined, and improperly built, is equally likely to end in disaster. Once in a while, during individual counseling sessions with either the husband or wife, the sad truth does, **eventually,** rise to the surface – their marriage began as a bad idea. It is one of the primary duties of the counselor, and especially the Christian counselor, to get the whole truth from each individual as quickly as possible, because **without the truth,** his or her hands are tied, and he or she cannot help either of the couple, much less salvage the relationship of the two. Please keep in mind here that the focus of this first chapter is still on **"mistakes"** – mistakes that happen **before** the wedding ceremony. And I must confess right here that I paused before going on with the next sentence. I paused, I hesitated, I blushed, and I prayed for guidance, because I have some statistics of my own, accumulated over forty years of ministry. I have kept a copy of every ceremony I performed in a file in the top drawer of my desk. Each time I open that drawer I am reminded of two faces, two human beings, standing in front of me, either reciting, reading, or repeating their vows to one another. Some of those couples are still together, happily married, with children and grandchildren of their own. Others have long since divorced, and re-married, some once, some twice, and others several times. A few have divorced and remained un-married till this day.

Among the couples whose marriages somehow "*got in trouble*", and who came to me for advice and/or counseling, there has been one truth, more than any other, when finally disclosed, that seems to be the worst culprit. This culprit will be dealt with in more detail in a later chapter – the chapter entitled **"*Intimacy*"**. In many circles nowadays, the term *intimacy*, has been almost lost in obscurity, and replaced with the modern, and seemingly more acceptable term – "***sex***". Someone asked – "*Is there a difference?*" My reply to that question is – "***If you have to ask if there is any difference between intimacy and sex, then I already know what your problem is.***"

In my experience with **"*troubled*"** marriages, this is where the trouble began, ***before*** the ceremony. In my own files, most of which I keep in my head instead of in a file cabinet, one of the persons (usually the woman,) eventually divulges the truth – her husband entered the marriage with one thing on his mind – sex! A few (very few,) husbands have, ***eventually,*** confessed that truth. Not in a single case have I ever heard an individual or couple say that the problem with their marriage was "***intimacy***" – it was always "***sex***". And here is where the marriage got in trouble, long before the couple stood in front of the minister. Either one, or both of the persons entering into this sacred institution, entered it with the ***wrong idea*** – the idea that marriage is all about the physical gratification of one or both of the individuals. A fellow minister came to me for advice on marriage counseling, telling me about an anonymous couple who were having "***sexual***" problems. My advice to him was to give the couple six words to memorize: "<u>***Sex is physical – intimacy is spiritual.***</u>" The young pastor thanked me for the advice, grinning as he left my office, replying – *"I never thought of it that way Pastor."*

    I have devoted less than seven pages to this profound topic entitled – Mistakes (please notice the "s"). Thus far I have dealt with only ***one*** mistake that occurs before the marriage takes place. Let me briefly deal with another more devastating mistake that has occurred, and is still occurring, in far too many marriages. I have said that the foundation is not the place to begin, but the very ***idea of marriage*** itself must be addressed before the foundation should be laid. A ***house*** is only as good as the ***materials*** from which is it fashioned, and the materials are only as good as the ***foundation*** upon which they are fastened, and a foundation is only as good as the ***idea*** or ideas that prompted its being laid, and an ***idea*** is only as good as the ***source*** from which it sprang. Not only is it possible for the ***idea*** to be all wrong, it is equally ***possible for the idea to spring from the wrong*** *source.*

A five-year-old child is not ready to propose the idea of building a house, and neither is he ready to propose marriage. Neither is a ten-year-old, nor a fifteen-year-old. And if any of you are silently asking at what age a man or woman is ready to propose marriage – there is no definitive, or universally-accepted answer. But let the author go on record as saying that far too many marriages should never have taken place for the simple reason - the parties involved were absolutely, positively ***too young and too immature*** to make that decision. And my files and the files of countless other ministers, counselors, and courts of law are inundated with facts and figures which prove it. And in addition to, and far transcending the cold, impersonal statistics, are the real, heart-wrenching confessions of those who have come to me, admitting they were totally unprepared for a marriage relationship, simply because they were ***too young*** to make that commitment.

At this point, the writer had to hesitate again, and do some serious soul searching before proceeding. Some of the saddest moments of my life have been those times when I had to sit down with couples and/or the parents of couples who got married too young, and listen to the heartbreaking stories of both the couples and their respective parents. But the most difficult moments of all were when I was asked for my advice as to whether the marriages, some which had lasted for a few years, and others which were on the brink of disaster, should continue, or be dissolved. It is in these tense and sometimes terrifying moments when the Pastor must tread lightly, reverently, and compassionately upon this sacred ground. But more than anything else, he must remain faithful to his Superior and to His Word.

While on a missionary trip to a third-world country with three other ministers, we were all asked by our host Pastor to speak to an assembly of two-hundred younger local ministers, many of whom had been waffling back and forth, halted between two opinions, not really certain whether they had been called to the ministry. The first preacher to speak was an elderly Pastor with many years of ministry to his credit. His first words, although not as well-received as any of us anticipated, rang with clarity, authority and effectiveness. As he gazed over the quiet assembly, he paused momentarily, clearing his throat, then saying – ***"Fellows, if you can do anything else – don't preach."*** And he sat down. There was a long silence. The old minister elbowed me in the side, letting me know it was now my turn to speak to the young men. As I rose to walk to the podium, I noticed many of those young men slowly walking away from the big tent, with their heads bowed low. They had finally gotten it settled in their hearts – they were not called to be preachers of the Gospel. Later that evening, in our hotel room, the older minister explained to me – *"If you can talk a man out of it - that, in itself, is the only evidence he needs to show him that he is not called of God."*

After much prayer, study, and seeking the advice of other more experienced Pastors than myself, I have often (with their permission,) employed some of the quaint sayings of some of those learned and highly-respected men in my own lectures, articles, sermons and books. For example, when I was much younger and inexperienced in the ministry, while having lunch with a dear elderly Pastor and friend, I asked for his advice. My question was – *"Pastor, what's the first thing I should say to a young couple who have come to me, asking me to perform their wedding ceremony?"* His response was quick, and, I must admit, a bit unexpected. Without a moment's hesitation, he replied – **"*Try to talk them out of it.*"** As he paused for effect, the effect sank in. If you can talk a young couple out of getting married - that, in itself, is the only evidence you need to show you, and them, that they are either too young, or simply not ready to be married. My files are filled with memories, many of which are still quite painful – memories of mothers and fathers (now in Heaven,) who, before they passed away, looked sadly into my face, telling me they had wished so many times that I had talked their sons or daughters out of getting married instead of *"marrying them"*. And yes, I have even had some couples themselves tell me later that they wished I had at least tried to talk them out of it years ago. And God only knows how many others are wishing that same thing at this very moment, but are unwilling to admit to each other, or to anyone else, that their marriage was a bad idea from the beginning.

It has always been my desire, and not just my duty, to be as fair and as kind to everyone as I can possibly be. And if I were to end this section of this book right here, it would not be fair to everyone concerned. But there is an even more compelling reason for me to continue this topic of "**mistakes**" that occur **before** the wedding ceremony, and that reason is that I must be true to my God, my conscience, my family, and to everyone else who may read these lines. There is another mistake, every bit as *fearful* and as *fatal* as any other, that is made **before** the ceremony. I call it the **ministerial mistake.** I have already alluded to this mistake in other comments, but I feel the need, the necessity, to elaborate a bit more.

If I may return to the analogy of a house and a

marriage again; in the same way a strong and beautiful house needs an ***architect*** with intelligence, intellect, integrity and experience, a marriage needs a ***minister*** with intelligence, intellect, integrity and experience. Like the architect who guards his reputation with vigilance, so must the minister vigilantly guard his reputation. And like the reputable architect who follows through on his plans, visiting the project in its infant stage, and onward to its completion, so should the ***faithful minister*** follow up on the couples whose ceremonies he performed, if possible, for as long as he is able to do so. At the risk of being challenged, or even criticized, let me say that the choice of a minister when planning a wedding is every bit as important (I believe more important,) as the choice of an architect when planning a house. No, it is not the minister who *"makes"* the marriage, and there are many who like to believe that the minister brings nothing to the marriage at all. And there is the mistake. **The minister must bring something to the marriage**, and if he doesn't, that, in itself, could be, and often is, a contributing factor in either the success or failure of the marriage.

    In my humble opinion, many ministers are as much to blame for the failure of some marriages as the individuals themselves, if not more so. Many ministers make one of two mistakes, either before or after the ceremony. Many failed marriages would never have taken place had the minister abstained from performing the ceremony in the first place. Some ministers are simply too eager to rush in – ***"where angels fear to tread".*** Some do it for the money; some do it for the honor bestowed upon them; and some do it as if what they say and do has no relevance to the union of the two persons standing in front of them. We are a society which too easily accepts the notion that the minister is nothing more than a figurehead. Were it not for the fact that the minister is required by law to sign the marriage license, in many cases, he is soon forgotten.

It might be quite interesting if a survey were to be taken, asking how many married couples remember the name of the minister who performed their ceremony, without looking at their marriage license. And how many couples remember anything the minister said during the ceremony? And why are the minister and his words so soon forgotten? Perhaps it is because he brought nothing to the marriage worthy of remembrance. How many ministers have we heard who, when teaching or preaching, loudly and adamantly proclaim that everything we do for God must be done in the power of the Holy Spirit? How many of us conclude our ceremonies with the words – "In the name of the Father, the

Son and the Holy Spirit?" I ask – How long has it been since you sensed the presence of the Holy Spirit at a wedding?

In forty years of ministry, it has been my unhappy lot to have to sit and listen to many a sermon, lecture and speech, many of which left me *cold*; others which left me *critical*, some which left me *confused*, and still others that left me *crying*. And the one factor which contributed most to my unhappy experience was the glaring absence of the Holy Spirit. A wedding ceremony, like any other aspect of ministry, performed without the unction of the Holy Spirit, is no different. There is *no warmth,* there is *no beauty*, there is no *sincerity*, and the saddest thing of all – there is *no witness* to the legitimacy of the union that is about to take place.

In all fairness, there are some couples who *do remember* the minister and his words – the words he spoke before, during, and after the ceremony. Yes, there have been some ceremonies performed with the unction of the Holy Spirit. And here is where this writer will possibly lose some friends, or the approval of some friends, or both. Those who remember both the minister and his words from their wedding ceremony do so because the minister brought something, (perhaps I should say *Someone*,) to the wedding – he brought the Holy Spirit to the wedding. I wish to go on record saying – *If the Holy Spirit did not marry you, you are not married. If the Holy Spirit did not marry you, your marriage is not legitimate. It may be legal in the eyes of the law, and acceptable to all parties involved, but it is not legitimate in the eyes of God.* Is it any wonder, then, that so many thousands (if not millions,) of marriages get in trouble, stay in trouble, and end in total disaster? Yet I dare not end this paragraph without giving the reader the basis of my argument. The Lord Jesus, when confronted by the self-righteous Pharisees about the legitimacy of *"putting away"*, or divorcing a wife, said –

For the hardness of your hearts he (Moses) wrote you this precept. But from the beginning of the creation God made them male and female. For this cause shall a man leave his father and mother, and cleave to his wife. And they twain shall be one flesh: so then they are no more twain, but one flesh. What therefore God hath joined together, let not man put asunder (Mark 10:5-9 KJV).

If I am not violating the rules of Scriptural interpretation, in the ninth verse, the Lord Jesus said that a true marriage is a marriage in which God Himself has joined the man and the woman. No two imperfect individuals, no imperfect minister, and no imperfect law can join two persons in *"holy"* matrimony. God, and God alone, is able to join men and women in holy matrimony. He joined Adam and Eve, and He alone knows how few or how many He has joined from that day to this. Will the reader pardon my audacity if I venture to say there have been fewer marriages performed by the Holy Spirit than by ministers, or those pretending to be ministers.

One of the saddest commentaries, and one of the most scathing indictments against ministers and their ministries today is that fact that so many couples are simply living together without being married, rather than have a ceremony performed by a minister, simply because they can't seem to find a minister with the integrity and trustworthiness to perform the ceremony. The fact that so many ministers have fallen into disgrace and reproach through their own ungodliness and flagrant, un-scriptural lifestyles, has given rise to countless numbers of ceremonies being performed by anyone who can order a *"ministerial license"* online.

I pray the reader can find it in his or her heart to bear with the writer if he dwells upon this point just a bit longer. I greatly fear that our society, and ministers themselves, place far too little emphasis upon the minister and his responsibilities in performing marriage ceremonies. When we perform marriage ceremonies, most ministers use a somewhat ***"standardized"*** or ***"traditional"*** rendition of the marriage vows, which the man and woman are asked to repeat after the minister. Some couples, of course, prefer writing their own vows, and reading them to each other at the ceremony, leaving the minister with little else to do but pronounce them man and wife. But in most *"traditional"* ceremonies, the bride and groom are asked to promise, or vow, that they will- love, honor, and cherish each other, and remain faithful to each other – ***"till death do you part"***, or ***"for as long as you both shall live".*** May I ask the reader - Which of these two vows would you prefer at your ceremony – *"till death do you part"*, or *"for as long as you both shall live"?* And is there any difference between the two? And while I must admit it would be very difficult, if not impossible, to differentiate between them, personally, I prefer the latter of the two. But be that as it may, and at the risk of being accused of *"splitting hairs"*, I find fault with both.

    Each of these vows – *"till death do you part"*, and *"for as long as you both shall live",* implies a limitation on every vow made. In other words, the word *"**till**"*, and the phrase *"**for as long**"*, imply - I will love you ***till*** one of us dies, but after that, I will not love you any longer; I will honor you ***for as long*** as we both shall live, but if you die before me, I will honor you no longer; and I will cherish you *till* death shall part us, but after that, I will cherish you no longer; and I will be faithful to you *for as long* as we both shall live, but if you die before me, I am not obligated to be faithful to you thereafter. Please do not misunderstand the writer here – I am not proposing that we re-write any part of the traditional wedding vows, and neither am I implying that there is something wrong, sinful, or inappropriate in a husband or wife being married a second time after the death of the spouse. The Holy Spirit was very clear in inspiring the writers of Scripture to allow for the needs and desires of fallen men and women who lose their spouse through death. But He was also just as clear in having the writers of Scripture set forth His own preference – that preference being that, however a marriage ends, whether through divorce or death, *it would be better, nay, it would be best,* for the man or woman to remain single thereafter. But these are things which are seldom, if ever, discussed between a couple and their minister before the ceremony.

We seem far more concerned with the ***ritualism of the ceremony*** than with the ***righteousness of the marriage.*** We seem far more concerned with the ***language of the ceremony*** than with the ***longevity of the marriage.*** But some of the godliest men and women I have ever known who lost their wife or husband through death have re-married, and have lived happily ever after. On the other hand, I have also known a few men and women who, after losing their spouse through death, remained unmarried for the rest of their lives. And these few who have remained unmarried have all, without exception, agreed upon one thing – that when their spouse died, half of their selves died also. Their loving, honoring, cherishing, and being faithful to their spouse did not end with the death of the spouse, and many of these dear saints grieved so deeply in the loss of their spouse, they soon followed their spouse in death, desiring to be where that loved one had gone.

  I had almost decided to end this section, and move on to mentioning several mistakes that are made in marriages ***after*** the ceremony takes place, but since we never know into whose hands our work will eventually fall, I feel it pertinent to our purpose to interject another major mistake which happens ***before*** many marriage ceremonies take place. It is a mistake which, if it were to be confessed by all who have made it, might far outnumber any or all of the others I have mentioned so far. I can only pray that no one who reads this small work has fallen into this trap. Perhaps the reader knows someone who has made this terrible mistake. It is simply the "***monetary mistake,***", or, as others might call it –

"marrying for money." Yes, it happens, and probably more often than we will ever know in this life, because it is the mistake that is less likely to be admitted than any other. How many persons have you heard confess that they married their spouse for their money?

In some cases the motive **seems** far more obvious than in others, but since we can never with 100% accuracy judge the motives of another person, we must leave all judgment to the righteous Judge who will someday bring all things into the light. It happens with men, it happens with women. It happens in all cultures, all countries, and within all ethnicities. Hollywood, of course, seems to add its own dimension to the madness in movies, films and "*sitcoms*". It seems our society is ready to accept just about any kind of relationship as long as it is endorsed, embraced, or condoned by the more liberal idealism of the Hollywood crowd.

I believe I have now mentioned four mistakes that are too often made before a wedding ceremony takes place – mistakes, which if avoided, might verily have prevented a life of unhappiness and all the other negative aspects that come with ***"jumping too soon."*** I pray that I have devoted relatively equal space to each of these mistakes. If the dear reader has not discarded the book by now, may I humbly beg your indulgence for a few more paragraphs?

There is yet another mistake which, if not taken seriously, can, and often does, allow a couple who are either too young or too immature to enter into a marriage contract to go ahead with their plans unadvisedly, then suffer the bitter consequences, sometimes for years, sometimes for a lifetime. I call this mistake *the parental mistake*. Please notice the writer did not indicate either a *"maternal"*, or *"paternal"* mistake, but a *"parental"* mistake. I will make no attempt to even insinuate that one parent has, or should have, more influence over the children than the other. If the influence of a mother happens to be greater than the influence of the father, or vice versa, it is **not necessarily** because the one is in any way a *"better"* parent than his or her mate. There are simply too many variables which come into play for anyone to make that assumption. In the ideal situation, both parents should have equal influence in the upbringing of their children. But, as the writer has already indicated, there are no *ideal,* or *perfect* marriages in this imperfect world. But, I must insist, there are some marriages that are far better than others, and I pray God will give me the wisdom to show what, or who, it is that makes the difference. We have all, no doubt, at one time or another, heard children characterized by the terms – *"mama's boy"*, or *"daddy's girl"*. These terms presuppose that one parent is *"**apparently**"* either more influential over the boy or girl, or that the boy or girl is *"**apparently**"* a bit closer to one parent than the other. I think the reader can read between the lines sufficiently to draw his or her own conclusions in either situation.

The point is – parents do have an influence over the destinies of their children. In an ever-changing world with ever-changing values and ideals that affect every area of our lives, is there any way we parents can be sure that our own personal influence over the lives of our children is more powerful than the many other forces with which they are bombarded every day? If we knew our child was too young to be thinking about marriage, but was adamantly insisting upon getting married, would our parental advice be enough to dissuade him or her from committing this terrible blunder? Could we *"**talk them out of it**"?* And would we if we could? Or would we adopt the sinister attitude of the modernistic movement, and let them plunge headlong into the abyss of an unholy relationship? If we love our children, we must never conform to the modernistic idea that a child has the right, or the capability, to make his or her own decisions. There is an age, a point, a time, at which they are capable and prepared to make decisions on their own, but the loving and discerning parent has both the God-given right and the

God-given responsibility of determining when that time has arrived.

Will the dear reader please pardon the writer one more time? I realize I intended to mention only five mistakes which happen before the marriage ceremony, but as I was about to close this section, yet another premarital mistake raised its ugly head, staring me in the face. I promise I will not spend too much time elaborating upon it. It is what I would call the "***perception***" mistake. Unfortunately, I am at a bit of a disadvantage here, simply because of the cold hard fact that in today's modernistic ideology, it has become acceptable in far too many cultures and countries for the man and woman to sleep together before the ceremony. I will spare the reader and myself the experience of describing all the details of what happens when lust overrides common sense. I ask, what beauty can there be, what intimacy can there be on the wedding night if the couple has already seen everything, and done everything?

But for those who are willing to wait until after the ceremony, let me share a paragraph or two about "***perception***". There she comes; her gown is glistening white; her teeth are white as snow; her hair shimmers in the light; the curves of her body are accentuated by the tight gown; underneath that gown is a woman whose body you have never seen (right?); her makeup is applied perfectly; her fingernails are well-manicured, and she comes toward you wearing a smile which lights up your world. She is healthy and happy. She is so near to perfection she makes your heart flutter with anticipation. And there you stand, straight and tall in your rented tuxedo, watching her every step. Underneath that tuxedo is a body she has never seen (right?). Your teeth are white as snow, your hair is well-groomed, your nails are clean and trimmed (hopefully), you are healthy and happy, and she gazes at her handsome prince who is so near to perfection he makes her heart flutter with anticipation. That is "***perception***".

It is only a matter of time until - she wakes up; her hair is disheveled; she has on no makeup; she is wearing faded pajamas; her teeth need brushing; her nails are neither painted nor manicured; she has gained some weight; there are children who must be awakened, groomed, fed, and sent to school; her health is failing, and she doesn't seem as happy as she was on her wedding day. And you – your hair is receding, or, like myself, you have wavy hair, most of which has waved goodbye; you have gained even more weight than your wife, and you must arise, brush your teeth, take a shower, groom whatever hair you have left, and go to work. There are bills to pay, a house and one or more vehicles that must be maintained, a family to feed, tuitions that must be paid, etc., etc., etc. That is *"reality"*.

What then? Shall the writer quit now, while he is still behind? Nay, he must go on, for the Holy Spirit will not allow him to quit here. Are you contemplating marriage? Are you old enough and mature enough to accept that responsibility, and make that lifelong commitment? Have you asked the Holy Spirit to guide you? Have you consulted the divine plan drawn by the divine Architect? Have you consulted a minister whose reputation, personality and character reflect the attributes of the Holy Spirit? Could someone like a friend, a relative, or a trusted minister or counselor talk you out of it? If you have considered all of the above, and are still confident that what you are about to do is sanctioned by the Holy Spirit, then by all means proceed, and may God bless your union. But if you have not, then by no means should you proceed any further until you know for a surety that God is in your plans, for if He is not in your plans, your idea, your dream, then neither will He be in your foundation, or your marriage.

Before proceeding to some of the mistakes that occur in a marriage **after the ceremony** and honeymoon are over, this poor writer must pause yet again, and beg the reader's patience and indulgence for a few more moments. In case any reader may question the motive behind the writing of this book (and he or she has every right to do so,) let me categorically assert that there is one, and only one, compelling motive that prompted the first and last words of this little book. It is the heart's desire and prayer of this author that somewhere in this book the reader will recognize his or her need to consult the Holy Bible as the first and final authority on all things spiritual. This writer probably hasn't written anything new or original on the subject of marriage, and will immediately proclaim that there are hundreds of other books out there which excel this one in both content and character – as far as the east is from the west. ***If this little book or any other book does not prompt or steer you toward the inspired, inerrant and infallible Word of God, then the writer has failed you miserably.*** God Himself is the Author and finisher of our faith, the Author of the Bible, and the Author of, and Authority on the subject of Marriage. He has magnified ***His Word*** above all ***His Name*** (Psalm 138:2) and it is ***there***, to His Word, that we must go if we would know the utmost truth on all spiritual matters, and Marriage is a ***spiritual matter***. It is by the standard of the Word of God that all other writings must either stand or fall, no matter who wrote them, or what they wrote in them.

Chapter Two

The "M" in Marriage = Mistakes!

It has been both my philosophy and my practice in ministry to avoid making the same mistakes which I counsel others to avoid. It has not been an easy thing to do at all times. Let the author of this little book openly confess here and now that he has made some mistakes both before and after his own marriage ceremony. He has learned from those mistakes, repented of them with a broken heart, and committed his life and marriage to the One who is more ready to forgive than to condemn. The downfall of many ministers and their ministries has been the fact that they themselves have engaged in many of the same sensual, sordid, and sometimes sadistic and sinister practices which they so adamantly preach against from the pulpit. If you, the reader, are anything like me, when you read or hear the words of another person who is preaching to you or giving you advice, you would like to believe that he or she has both the authority and the integrity to justify giving advice to others. We want our preachers and teachers to practice what they preach – at all times. If we would be honest, we would have to admit that we would like for our ministers to be as close to perfection as a man can get in all matters. We want him to be above reproach. And can anyone measure the degree of disappointment we feel if or when we discover that the man who has been preaching to us has been found guilty of the same sins he has told us to avoid?

If a minister has taken it upon himself to teach or preach on such a sacred subject as Marriage, we have the right to expect, nay, to demand that he be above reproach in that area. And if the reader is questioning how we can know whether our counselor is above reproach, there are at least *four tests* by which we can discern his integrity, or absence thereof. First of all, and most importantly, does the Holy Spirit bear witness to his words? Secondly, do his words agree with the Holy Scriptures? Thirdly, does he have a good report from all who know him, or does his walk match his talk? And fourthly, what effect, if any, does his teaching have upon us? If a man's preaching and teaching has no effect whatsoever upon your life, you have no reason, and no responsibility to listen to, or follow him or his teaching. If any of these four elements is absent, we have both *the right* and *the responsibility* to reject both him and his teaching.

Let us never diminish the degree of sanctity which the Lord Himself has placed upon and into this sacred institution of Marriage, and let us not tarnish that sacred image of purity which He has stamped upon it. And let us not endeavor to justify ourselves by deliberately misinterpreting, misapprehending, or misappropriating His Word on the subject. And this brings the author to that point which he desperately wanted to avoid at the beginning of this book. I wanted to confine myself to those mistakes that are made *before a marriage ceremony*, and leave the others (those made afterward,) to the more intelligent and more qualified men and women who are far more capable than myself. I have engaged in much prayer, and in great searchings of my own heart, experience, and acquaintance with the Word of God before going forward with this study. And after much deliberation, and in the spirit of humility and reverence, I cannot in good conscience dismiss the compulsion of my heart to at least mention one or two of those horrible mistakes which have happened, and are happening, in far too many marriages, *after the ceremony*.

This first mistake I am about to mention presented me with a bit of difficulty in naming it. I finally settled on the title – *momentary mistakes* in marriage. I went to my trusty dictionary to make sure I was using the most fitting definition of the term – *momentary*. One of the definitions of the term is…likely to happen any moment, or in a moment. Now let that sink in for a moment. In my many years of being a Pastor and counselor, listening to the stories of broken homes, broken hearts, and broken lives, I've learned that a great number of the mistakes made by either the man or the woman - mistakes which led to heated arguments, or eventually to separation or divorce, **happened in a single moment**.

If you are a serious student of the Scriptures, perhaps this has steered your mind toward the story of David and Bathsheba, as recorded in the Book of II Samuel, chapters eleven and twelve. In a single moment, a decision, a choice was made which has affected virtually the whole world to some degree. David was a married man, and Bathsheba was a married woman. Either of them could have prevented this horrible act from happening. David could have denied his lust, and Bathsheba could have denied David his passion, but neither of them denied the other, and their sin, and the results of their sin have been preached probably more often than any other sin ever committed, with the possible exception of Adam and Eve eating the forbidden fruit. And let us not forget – these things were written for our learning. Yes, it took more than a moment for David and Bathsheba to commit the act of adultery, but it only took a moment for them to decide to do it. I doubt that there is a serious and honest student of the Scriptures who would disagree with me if I say that **the cost** of that *"mistake"*, that sin, is positively immeasurable. But let us never forget - David's decision to commit adultery with Bathsheba was made **before the physical act** took place in the royal bedroom. In fact, David made some serious mistakes before he even looked at the bathing beauty. Perhaps this little four-line poem might deter someone from making the same momentary mistake David made:

> With his eyes he looked,
> And his heart was hooked;
> The date was booked,
> And his goose was cooked.

Momentary mistakes are indeed costly, both in marriages and in everyday life, to both the believer and the infidel. In the twentieth chapter of the Book of Numbers, we have the sad account of Moses, one of the greatest leaders of the Old Testament, committing a sin unto death, simply because, in a single moment, he failed to glorify his God in the eyes of the people, smiting the rock with his rod, after God had told him to speak to the rock. By that momentary decision, and the act that followed, he forfeited the blessing of entering the promised land of Canaan, and died on Mount Nebo. How many marriages have been destroyed because one person, in a single moment, in a fit of anger, jealousy, or ignorance, lashed out at his or her spouse without stopping to consider the consequences of their actions? And how many more marriages have suffered because either the man or his wife – *"looked the other way"* for a moment, instead of keeping their eyes straight ahead?

The Scriptural examples this writer could use to illustrate the impact and extent of these momentary mistakes could fill hundreds of pages. But this is now 2017, and the reader may be asking how all of this is relevant to today, and what is happening in marriages today. It is no different today than it was over three-thousand years ago. Men and women are making these same momentary mistakes over and over again, 24 hours a day, 365 days a year. Marriages are crumbling, nay, dissolving every day simply because someone made a foolish decision in a single moment, and acted upon that decision. How high is the cost of a momentary mistake? I, for one, say the cost is too high. Once committed, it can never be reversed, it can never be undone, and the sad effects, the consequences of it reach farther than any author's pen can write. History proves that the effects of David's decision are being felt to this day. His descendants have had to live by the sword from that day to this, just as God said they would. Why, then, do men and women still insist upon acting upon these momentary decisions? There are only two possible answers. (1) They either ***do not know what the Word of God teaches on the sanctity of marriage,*** or (2) they know it, ***and yet neglect or reject that teaching.***

I am finding it very difficult to bring this section of the book to a close. My mind wants to go on to another topic, but my heart won't allow it. I suppose it's the Pastor in me that won't allow me quit here. It would not be fair to the reader for me to leave out anything that might be profitable to him or her. Just recently, in a Wednesday night Bible study, I was asked to comment on the teaching of another Pastor – teaching which left some of his students a bit confused, and some even frustrated. He simply got off the subject at hand, and began rambling aimlessly through the Scriptures. It seemed as if his mind was not engaged with his mouth, and nothing he was saying seemed to be connected with the subject matter. I wanted to be as compassionate as possible with him, and yet not leave the questions of the students unanswered.

Finally, as if in answer to my silent prayer, the Pastor himself confessed that he had lost his train of thought, and asked me if I would bring the lesson back to its proper context. The teaching was about ***temptation,*** and the ***consequences*** of giving in to temptation. My heart immediately went to the Garden of Gethsemane, where our Lord prayed in such an agony His sweat became as great drops of blood falling to the ground. He was a mere stone's cast away from his inner circle of disciples – Peter, James, and John. But just before He withdrew from them to enter into prayer, he cautioned them…Pray that ye enter not into temptation (Luke 22:40b). It seems they either didn't hear Him, or they heard, and yet ignored His words, because when He came back to them, they were asleep. I can only hope that they prayed before they fell asleep, for the Scripture is silent on the matter. But the fact is, when He came to them, He again said virtually the same thing He had said before He walked away…Why sleep ye? rise and pray, lest ye enter into temptation (Luke 22:46).

    Can you not see the picture? Here are three men who are to later change the world with their preaching and teaching. But before they are prepared to be the men they are to become, they must be taught by the Master. And one of the first and most valuable lessons they must learn from Him is the necessity of vigilant prayer. With the Lord Himself only a few yards away, they are susceptible to temptation – temptation which can, and will exert itself in less than the time it takes for a man to walk a few yards, and even while they are asleep! Yes, that's how subtle temptation is, and that's how quickly temptation creeps in – it is momentary, meaning it can happen at any moment, and in a moment. And temptation calls for a decision – a Yes, or a No. And it takes no longer time, and no more effort to make a wise choice than to make a foolish one. Please allow me to illustrate the point with another true story from more recent times.

A Pastor in California received a phone call from a divorced lady in his congregation. She sounded quite desperate, begging the Pastor to come as soon as possible to talk to her. The Pastor's wife was in another state, visiting her sick Mother. The Pastor had already asked his entire congregation never to ask him to come and visit a single lady, a divorced lady, or a young widow unless there could be someone else present wherever the meeting was to take place. He quickly informed the young divorcee that he simply could not come and visit her alone. But the young and very attractive divorcee began to cry on the phone, begging the Pastor to please come and talk to her, assuring him her young son would be there, so the two of them would not have to be alone. Against his better judgment, the Pastor reluctantly agreed to visit her with the stipulation that her son must be either in the same room or at least within earshot of them when they talked. The young lady agreed to his terms.

When he arrived and rang the doorbell, the young lady (let's call her Evelyn,) was in the bedroom. Hearing the doorbell, she called out – *"It's open Pastor, come on in."* Pastor Johnson's every instinct told him he should not have come here, and that he should leave immediately. He was thinking about turning and walking away when Evelyn called out again – *"Be right there Pastor."* When she opened the door, Pastor Johnson gasped. There she stood, wearing a tight-fitting dress that accentuated every curve of her shapely body. The hemline was more than half way up her thighs, revealing most of her long, silky-smooth legs, and the neckline left very little to the imagination. Her perfume smelled very sensual, her honey-blonde hair flowed down to her waist, her lips were painted a deep red, and her voice was soft and low. As Pastor Johnson prayed silently for guidance, Evelyn turned and walked toward the plush sofa, sitting down, crossing her legs. The tight dress rode up even higher on her legs.

Pastor Johnson could read her expression, and her body language. He was nobody's fool. He had been put in this situation before – something Evelyn didn't know. Something else she didn't know about Pastor Johnson was that he loved his wife, he loved his family, he loved his church, and he loved his Lord. It wasn't very difficult to discern what she wanted from Pastor Johnson, but she was about to learn that some men are not as easily seduced as others. Inside the house less than a minute, he stood just inside the front door. As he looked sternly into her face she quickly un-crossed her legs, trying to hide as much of her legs as she could with her hands. Pastor Johnson calmly but firmly told her – *"Mrs. Frakes, you have called me here with less than honorable intentions, and I do not appreciate it at all. This is very unbecoming of a lady who professes to be a Christian, and I will have no part of it."*

Evelyn had embarrassed herself. Whatever it was she had expected from Pastor Johnson, she knew she was not going to get. She bowed her head, asking him to forgive her for her actions. He assured her he could forgive her immediately, but added that she should probably ask forgiveness from someone else. Her face turned pale. As Pastor Johnson turned to leave, Evelyn stood up, taking a few steps toward him. Her last words were – *"All I can say Pastor is that your wife must be some kind of woman."* He smiled, tipping his hat, replying – *"That she is Ma'am, that she is."*

Perhaps the reader is now congratulating Pastor

Johnson for making one of those momentary *wise* decisions, instead of a *foolish* one. Was he tempted? Did he contemplate having a quick affair with a gorgeous young divorcee? I humbly submit to you – Pastor Johnson had his mind made up before he went to see Mrs. Frakes. Neither she, nor any other woman, regardless of her age or appearance, could have gotten him to betray his wife, his family, his church, or his Lord. His decision to reject her advances was made *before he left his home*. In closing this chapter, that is exactly the point the writer wishes to emphasize – **he made his decision beforehand.**

I have strongly emphasized earlier that any author who is worth his salt will quickly steer the reader away from his own work, and toward the Word of God. I believe I also stated that if the writer does not steer the reader toward the Word of God, he has failed you miserably. May I add one more note in that same vein of thought. It is my own humble opinion that if the writing of any author does not attempt to steer you into God's Word, then the writing of that author is probably not worth what you paid for it, and you should quickly discard it. Let me illustrate from the Word of God how our blessed Lord Jesus dealt with His own temptations.

When we read of the temptation of Christ in the wilderness, or when we listen to most preachers preach on that subject, we are often given only those three temptations which are recorded in Matthew 4, and Luke 4. If the reader will notice, when the tempter came to Jesus, he proposed – (a) turning stones into bread, (b) leaping from a pinnacle of the temple, and finally, (c) bowing down and worshiping the devil. Has the reader ever noticed how quickly and summarily our Lord dismisses each temptation with a quote from the Word of God? The battle is over almost as quickly as it began – one, two, three, and the temptations are over. Have you ever wondered, or even considered what the Word of God teaches – **before** these three final temptations were proposed by the devil? Luke, inspired by the Holy Spirit, tells us:

And Jesus being full of the Holy Ghost returned from Jordan, and was led by the Spirit into the wilderness, Being forty days tempted of the devil…(Luke 4:1,2a).

Jesus was tempted for forty days and forty nights – **before** these last three temptations came to Him. He was able to quickly dismiss all three temptations because He had already endured forty days and forty nights of temptation beforehand. When these last three temptations came, His mind was already made up – He would not succumb to the devil's advances. And here is a twofold lesson for us. First, like any other worthwhile exercise, the more we resist temptation, the better we become at it. When we have successfully overcome a powerful temptation, the next one may be as powerful, or even more so than the last, but having conquered the first, we are far better prepared for the next. And secondly, and I believe more importantly, if we prepare ourselves, *if we equip ourselves beforehand*, whether the source of the temptation is the world, the flesh, or the devil, or all of these, they stand little chance of making us their victim. The Word of God teaches that we have a great High Priest, Who was - in all points tempted like as we are, yet without sin (Hebrews 4:15b). Our Lord Jesus was tempted…in all points…like as we are. Have we been tempted to commit adultery? Then Jesus, in His flesh, must necessarily have known the full impact of that same temptation. Have we been tempted to steal? Then Jesus was tempted to steal. He was tempted, He was tested, He was tried, and He was triumphant. It is my deep conviction that many, or most, of those points in which He was tempted came to Him during that forty days and forty nights in the Judean wilderness. It is also my deep conviction that He was tempted even while on the Cross – a point which I have strongly emphasized in another book entitled – Giving the Devil His Due.

    It may not true of every man and woman that he or

she endured more and stronger temptations when they were single than they endured after marriage, but in my forty-nine years of marriage and forty years of ministry, it has been my personal experience, and that of nearly every individual and couple who have spoken with me in private, that all of us have endured far more temptations after we were married than before we were married. If the world, the flesh, and the devil are unable to seduce a young man or woman into lasciviousness while they are single, that is a good sign, a good indication, and a good testimony to the character of the individual. But let no man or woman be lulled into the complacent notion that temptations will cease after marriage, because they will not. In fact, they are likely to increase in both number and strength after marriage. It is a godly marriage the devil hates most, and he will stop at nothing in an attempt to infiltrate and infect that marriage, and his temptations are engineered to lure either the man or the woman, or both, into a momentary lapse in judgment, a moment in which he is able to make just the right insinuation that will best serve his evil purpose.

When we make those momentary mistakes, it is because we have not prepared and equipped ourselves in prayer and studying the Word of God. With God's Word hidden in our hearts, and having been in close communion with our Lord in prayer, the devil is no match for us. In fact, he will flee from us. But let us never forget – he will be back again and again, and probably sooner than later. I close this chapter with a simple reminder – temptation is a powerful thing, but it is also a passing thing. I did not say it is *passive*, but passing, and there is a difference. Temptation is powerful, but it is not permanent. It comes and goes. And if you do not know the Lord Jesus Christ as your personal Savior, you have nothing but your own will power with which to resist temptation, and your will, like all your other faculties, is depraved, twisted out of a straight line, and incapable of dealing with temptation in the same strength of a born again believer. How you deal with temptation can mean the difference between life and death, Heaven and Hell. The married man or woman who is unable, or unwilling, to resist temptation, and succumbs to it, makes that momentary mistake, the consequences of which often last for a lifetime. And seldom do the mistakes, the sins of one person affect only the one who commits them. Far too often, there are several persons affected, and as most ministers and counselors agree, it's usually the children who suffer most. And another thing on which virtually all Christian ministers agree is – the Bible will keep you from sin, or sin will keep you from your Bible. And that brings us to the next chapter – the first "a" in Marriage, which stands for "***authority***".

Chapter Three

The "a" in Marriage = Authority

Here is where we must be the most reverent, and here is where we must be the most cautious in our thinking and our acting. Many a heated controversy has sprung from the simple fact that men and women either neglect or reject the clear teaching of Scripture. Since the fall of Adam, men and women have argued (probably every day) over the question of who has the final authority in a Marriage. Actually, there should be no controversy at all as to who is the first and final authority in the sacred institution of Marriage. This could and should be the shortest chapter in this book, but I seriously doubt that it will be, because we live in an imperfect world, blighted by sin, and steeped in ignorance of the Word of God. Men of corrupt minds have taken it upon themselves to re-define the sacred terms in that great Book. Terms like **marriage**, **sacred,** and **intimacy** have suffered much at the hands of men and women who have little or no knowledge of their meaning, and little or no respect for the dignity of each term.

    I will waste no time in getting straight to the point. There is one, and only one Authority in a marriage, and that Authority is the perfect, infallible, inerrant, inspired Word of God. It is the perfect plan, drawn by the perfect Architect, and given to the world through the Prophets and Apostles. When a reputable architect delivers his plans to the builder, he expects the builder to follow the plan. The builder may or may not do as the architect intended for him to do. In fact, it is entirely possible that neither the builder nor the person or persons who are to occupy the house know the architect personally, on a first name basis. If the builder and/or occupant of the house have not followed the plan of the architect, that does not mean there was something wrong with the plan or the architect who drew it up – it means his written instructions were not followed. Let me quickly add – it is my deep conviction that the whole project would run a lot smoother, and end up far better if all parties concerned knew each other personally, and had at least a working knowledge of the plan for the building. And so it is in a Marriage. All the parties involved should know each other personally, and have a working knowledge of the Plan.

    Let us not mince our words here, and let us not beat around the bush, nor sidestep the issue for the sake of expediency or self-approval. It is quite clear that, in the beginning of the institution of Marriage, the man and the woman were equal partners, with neither being superior or inferior to the other in any form, or to any degree. That was the original plan! It was not until after sin entered the Garden that a different plan was announced, and let us not forget who made the announcement. With the entrance of sin into the human soul, God Himself stepped in, took the matter into His own hands, and introduced His new plan for Marriage – a plan which He has never abrogated or abandoned from that day to this. He made the man the head of the woman, period. This is a status, of course, which too many men take too seriously, and which an even greater number of men do not take seriously enough. Before the couple sinned, they were the perfect couple, with no inhibitions, and no prohibitions as far as their relationship to each other was concerned. We know, of course, there was one, and only one, prohibition – the eating of the forbidden fruit. But the moment sin invaded man's being, everything changed. Adam could no longer be the perfect husband, and Eve could no longer be the perfect wife. And the eternal mind of God (the Authority,) determined that one of them (the man) must be the head, the leader, and the example to the other.

In Genesis 3:16 God specifically said to the woman:

I will greatly multiply thy sorrow and thy conception: in sorrow thou shalt bring forth children; and thy desire shall be to thy husband, ***and he shall rule over thee.*** (Italics mine)

I have seen many ladies, both married and single, cringe when that verse was quoted, and I have seen many men, both married and single, gloat when they heard it. Women have no reason to cringe or go on the defensive at this verse, and neither do men have any reason to gloat, or get all puffed up with pride when this verse is quoted. And why not? Because these words proceeded out of the mouth of God, and, as the Scripture teaches – man shall not live by bread alone, but by every word that proceedeth out of the mouth of God. The words in Genesis 3:16 are words to live by as much as the words in John 3:16 are words to live by. Far too many women have ***rebelled against the authority*** of these words, and I greatly fear that far too many men have ***misinterpreted the authority*** of these words. The thing that most men seem to forget, (and they forget it easily,) is that, ***with authority comes responsibility***. But before the reader gets the wrong idea here, let me clarify what I'm trying to say.

Question: Did God make Adam the authority in the marriage relationship? Answer: Yes, He did. But what kind of authority was it with which God invested the man? First of all, any kind or degree of authority with which God may have invested the man is, at best, *a secondary authority* – secondary to **God's own authority**, which is His infallible Word. The first and final authority which is to govern the marriage relationship was, is, and forever shall be, God's Word. And right here, at the risk of alienating, or even losing some friends, the writer must follow his convictions. It is my conviction that in order for any man to have the right to be the head of his wife and family, he must first have God as ***his*** head, and God's Word as ***his authority***. And in order to have God as his head, and God's Word as his authority, he must be personally and intimately acquainted with both. Show me the man who is not well-acquainted with God and his Word, and I will show you a man who is not well-qualified to be a husband and father.

And secondly, both the man and the woman heard what God said. How, then, would each of them interpret what God said? It becomes crystal clear when we …rightly divide the word of truth! Please note that when God created the man, He gave him ***dominion*** over all the earth – over all cattle, the fish of the sea, the fowl of the air, and every creeping thing. ***Nowhere*** in the Bible is it written that God gave the man ***dominion*** over the woman. To rule is one thing, to have dominion is another. *Ruling* and *dominating* are two different terms, with different definitions. Allow the writer to use two illustrations, both of which, I believe, show how God may have intended Adam and Eve to understand His words…he shall rule over thee.

First, I have already stated that, when Adam sinned, everything changed. And when I say everything, I mean everything in the natural, physical, spiritual, and moral realms. It did not take long for the horrific effects of sin to manifest themselves in each of these realms – the murder of Abel at the hand of his brother being just one visible effect. As the cost of the sin of David cannot be measured, neither can the cost of the sin of Adam be measured – **until we look at the Cross**. And as Adam's sin changed everything for the worse, so Christ's death and resurrection changed everything for the better. But did everything, or anything within the marriage relationship change with the death and resurrection of Christ? Perhaps I should go one step farther before attempting to answer that question. We cannot base our argument upon only the death and resurrection of Christ – we must also include His ascension to the right hand of the Father, where He, as the great High Priest of his people, ever lives to make intercession for them.

The beloved Apostle Paul, in the fifth chapter of Ephesians, within twelve verses (22-33), gives us what this writer believes to be the perfect pattern for a loving and lasting marriage relationship. If you, the reader, have not already opened your Bible since you began reading this little book, you should open it now! In verses 22-24 of this chapter (chapter 5,) we read:

Wives, submit yourselves unto your own husbands, as unto the Lord. For the husband is the head of the wife, even as Christ is the head of the church: and he is the savior of the body. Therefore as the church is subject unto Christ, so let the wives be to their own husbands in everything.

He specifically addresses the wife here, and her God-given duty toward her husband. After Calvary, after the empty tomb, and after His ascension to Heaven, centuries after Eden and The Law, the husband is still...the head of the wife. And unless I have missed something, this arrangement has not changed since the close of the New Testament. No, I am not being a chauvinistic male, I am simply stating what the Holy Spirit had the Apostle to write. ***But lest I should lose my audience in a single moment, please be patient, and allow me to qualify what I have written. The husband being the head of the wife – <u>DOES NOT APPLY IN ALL CASES.</u> In fact, the principle of the*** *man being the head of the woman has never applied to every married couple in any age, since the fall of Adam. It is my firm conviction that the principle of the man being the head of the woman is, and always has been, a <u>conditional principle</u>. No man anywhere in the world has either the right or the privilege of calling himself the head (the authority,) of his wife and family until he himself can call God his head, and God's Word his authority. A man who has never submitted and committed his life to Jesus Christ, and has no working knowledge of the Holy Bible, has no God-given right to call himself an authority, head, or ruler.* This becomes clearer with Paul's next admonition – to the husband, beginning at verse 25, where he writes:

Husbands, love your wives, even as Christ also loved the church, and gave himself for it; That he might sanctify and cleanse it with the washing of water by the word. That he might present it to himself a glorious church, not having spot, or wrinkle, or any such thing; but that it should be holy, and without blemish. So ought men to love their wives as their own bodies. He that loveth his wife loveth himself. For no man ever yet hated his own flesh; but nourisheth and cherisheth it, even as the Lord the church: For we are members of his body, of his flesh, and of his bones. For this cause shall a man leave his father and mother, and shall be joined unto his wife, and they two shall be one flesh. This is a great mystery: but I speak concerning Christ and the church. Nevertheless let every one of you in particular so love his wife even as himself; and the wife see that she reverence her husband.

Did anyone else notice that the Holy Spirit inspired Paul to write only three verses to the wife, and nine verses (three times as many) to the husband? And we haven't even gotten to any of the other Apostle's writings on the subject of Marriage yet! This poor writer deliberately used the first "a" in Marriage to stand for *"authority"* for a reason. But men's reasons and motives for writing whatever they write, regardless of how noble their intentions may be, can never reach the length, breadth, depth and height of divine inspiration and *authority* as the inspired pens of the men who wrote the Bible. We are, all of us, no more than mortal commentators upon the divinely inspired Word of God, and we can never become anything more than that, regardless of our education, training, or number of degrees that follow our names. In fact, this same inspired Apostle – Paul, tells us in Romans 3:4 that we are to…let God be true, but every man a liar. Here, God emphatically puts all men in their place – their proper place.

If we can agree that the Word of God is *the first and*

final authority on all things relevant to human existence, then, and only then, are we able to proceed, and walk together as men of God. The moment we begin to relegate God and His Word to a secondary position, behind, beneath, or to any degree less than Who and What they are, and replace ***His authority*** with ***man's authority***, we have, in essence, made ourselves our own God, and our words superior to His words.

Paul's first words to the husband are…Husbands, love your wives, even as Christ also loved the church, and gave Himself for it:

Does this poor student of the Scriptures really need to go any farther than this in order to establish his argument? The first condition which the man must meet in order to establish himself as the head of the wife is that he must love her ***in the same manner,*** (and to the extent of giving his life for her,) ***the same degree*** that Christ loves his bride – the church. Anything less than this immediately disqualifies him as the head of the wife, and renders him powerless, with absolutely no degree of God-given authority. It matters not how many other conditions he may meet, if he does not meet this one first, ***he cannot be the authority*** in his marriage.

Since I began writing this book, there have been countless interruptions and obstacles which have greatly hindered the work. One of those obstacles has been my own sense of incompetence and unworthiness to write such a book in the first place. But my dear patient wife, Carolyn, and a dear friend, Eva Dimel, herself a noted author and poet, have been a great source of encouragement, always encouraging me to continue writing. Today, April 21st, 2017, I told my wife that I had now reached that *"point of no return"*, meaning I have now committed myself to finishing the task I began about two months ago. Under normal circumstances, without a great deal of interruptions, I have completed some of my books in less than three months. With this book, I have almost twenty-eight pages which have taken me more than two months to write. This book will take a while to complete, because it is one of the most important projects I have ever undertaken.

In one of my more than 230 poems – a poem entitled "Words", in the last line of that poem, I wrote – *"but let my tongue be silent if it honors not my Lord."* May the same be true of our computers, our phones, our social media, and any and all other means by which we communicate, verbally, or on the written page. In beginning this book, I deliberately chose the verse – Hebrews 13:4 for a specific reason. There were many other verses I could have chosen, and many I could have included with this verse at the beginning, but I decided to let that verse stand alone at the head of this book – Marriage is honorable in all, and the bed undefiled: but whoremongers and adulterers God will judge.

But what does the Holy Spirit mean when He says…Marriage is honorable in all? First of all, Marriage is honorable to God Himself; God Himself honors Marriage, because Marriage, Scriptural Marriage, honors God. A Marriage that honors God is honored by God, because it makes Him the head and authority in that relationship. Secondly, Marriage honors God's Word, and since God and His Word are inseparable, a Marriage which honors God's Word, honors the Author of that Word. God has invested His Word with all of His authority. He will do absolutely nothing that is contrary to His Word, which makes His Word the absolute and final authority in all matters governing human relationships. Marriage, then, honors God, meaning, of course, all the three Persons of the Godhead, the Father, the Son, and the Holy Spirit. Marriage honors His Word, it honors the man and the woman entering into its sacred chamber, and it honors the human race, fallen as the race may be.

The beloved Sarah, the wife of Abraham, had no problem in following Abraham's leadership, even calling him lord, **because Abraham had made God his Lord first**.

Abraham was *lord and leader of his* home because he was first *the light of his home*. Sarah could see God in Abraham. Did Abraham make mistakes? Of course he did. He, like countless other husbands, made a few of those momentary mistakes, mistakes which cost him and his posterity immeasurable pain and suffering. But he was still God's man, and the one thing, more than any other, which made Abraham the man he was, was the simple fact that he…believed God. He believed that whatever promise God made, no matter how distant the fulfillment of the promise might be, God would bring His Word to pass without fail. After a few hard-learned lessons, he let God's Word be ***the authority*** in his life and marriage.

In more than forty years of ministry, it has been my delight to see a few Marriages which mirror the teaching of God's Word. And in each of those Marriages, I see the woman and the man gathered around God's Word, studying together, praying together, and staying together. I have had the honor of baptizing their children – children which they themselves led to Christ. And these couples require no counseling from their Pastor, because they have allowed God's Word to be their Counselor, their guide, their daily bread, and their first and final authority on all matters. Couples like these are a joy to serve. They are the couples who inspired this Pastor to entitle the next chapter of this book...

Chapter Four

The "rr" in Marriage = Railroad.

You've never heard of a railroad Marriage? Neither had I until I began writing this book! Many years ago I worked for the railroad for about eight months. I was in a group called an "extra gang", taking up the old rails, and replacing them with new ones. I learned a lot of valuable lessons in that short time – lessons which have served me well in the ministry and in my Marriage. First of all, the work we did was hot, hard, and backbreaking. We went for long periods in the blistering sun without any water to drink. We ate greasy food cooked in a makeshift kitchen car, and we slept in a railroad car with no air conditioning the whole summer, with temperatures reaching 104 degrees. I saw several young men fall by the side of the tracks from heat exhaustion and dehydration. Sometimes we were so far out in the countryside, the only water we had to drink was from a nearby stream. We had no idea if it was safe to drink or not, but we drank it anyway, rather than die of thirst.

A railroad, much like a Marriage, is a very interesting piece of engineering. Granted, the differences between the two probably far outnumber the similarities, but, be that as it may, there are some very striking similarities between a well-built railroad and a well-built Marriage. The railroad, like a Marriage, has a bed (a foundation) upon which it rests. The railroad bed itself must be laid with some degree of precision and foresight in order to hold the huge wooden crossties in place. On top of the wooden crossties are steel plates with square holes on each side. The rail is laid in the center of the steel plate, and heavy spikes, sharp on one end and having a large head are driven through the holes into the crossties. The heads of the four spikes hold the rail in place.

Most of this process is now done by hydraulic machines powered by either gasoline or diesel fuel. But the hardest, backbreaking work is still done by hand, some of which includes pulling the spikes out of the ties, lifting the steel plates off to the side, then putting them back when the crew is ready for the new rail to be put in place. Then there is the driving of the spikes the machine missed. This work requires that a man spend eight to ten hours a day bent over in the hot sun, lifting steel plates, first off the ties, then back onto the ties.

Marriage requires a lot of hard work also. It may not be as arduous and backbreaking as working on a railroad, but it is work, and sometimes it can be exhausting for both the husband and the wife, especially if there are children to tend to. But Marriage, like a railroad, has its beautiful and symmetric qualities also. The rails both run in the same direction at all times, no matter how far they reach. And no matter where they go, and no matter how much heat or cold the two rails endure, they are never far apart. In fact, the space between the two rails is virtually the same at all times. And if one rail does move away from the other, it is only a fraction of an inch. A railroad is engineered so that the two rails are, from all appearances, identical in nature, and the distance between them is maintained with virtually imperceptible variation.

A railroad, like a Marriage, responds in certain ways to forces both inside and outside itself. Before the advent of thermonuclear welding, the rails were joined by steel plates on each side of the joint, with steel bolts going though the plates and the rail itself. But there had to be a gap between the adjoining rails to allow for expansion in high temperatures. When the temperature drops, the rails contract, returning to their original length, leaving that little gap exactly the same size it was before the expansion took place.

If the gap wasn't there, the heat expansion would cause the rails to buckle at the joint, derailing the next train that came along. This heating and cooling, and the expansion and contraction of a steel rail happens slowly, imperceptibly. Many a horrible and costly accident has been prevented because someone had the ingenuity to discover how steel reacts to heat and cold.

    I am told that after long periods of extreme heat, which causes two joined rails to expand, and then contract again and again when the heat subsides, the rails become just a little bit weaker each time this happens. After years of this expanding and contracting, that joint is no longer safe for a train to roll across it, and must be replaced with new rails. And the point at which the two rails are joined is the weakest point of the entire rail. If you have ever observed a railroad track while a train is speeding across the rails, you can see the place where two rails are joined rising and falling, while the rest of the rail remains immoveable. Each time one of the train wheels passes over the joint, the joint falls perhaps as much as an inch or two. As soon as the wheel passes the joint, the joint rises up again. This rising and falling happens every time another wheel passes over the joint. This rising and falling from the pressure, the weight of the train, hundreds, or even thousands of times a day, coupled with the heating and cooling, expanding and contracting, loosens the nuts and bolts, weakening the joint, and the rails themselves. If the bolts are not re-tightened, the rails will soon go out of alignment, and when that happens, disaster is imminent. Simply put, **where** the two rails are joined is not nearly as important as **how** they are joined. And so it is with any Marriage. The place **where** the Marriage ceremony takes place is not nearly as important as **how** the ceremony takes place.

A Marriage must make some allowances and adjustments due to the many forces both inside and outside itself. The laws of physics demand that a steel rail expand and contract in response to heating and cooling. The laws of Marriage demand that the man and his wife respond a certain way to certain forces, lest the Marriage buckle, and a horrible and costly disaster ensue. And as the unseen forces that cause a steel rail to expand and contract work slowly and imperceptibly, so do the forces, both seen and unseen, that cause a Marriage to buckle, work slowly, and often imperceptibly. The joining of two persons in holy matrimony, like the joining of two steel rails, if not performed properly, is a recipe for disaster.

In the same way that a steel chain is only as strong as its weakest link, the railroad – the entire length of it, is only as strong as its weakest point. By its very design, the weakest point in a steel rail is at the point where two rails are joined. The many different forces, natural and physical forces which so often exert themselves upon that joint render it vulnerable and susceptible to further weakening. If you were to ask ten different persons what is the weakest point in a marriage, you would probably get ten somewhat different answers. And it probably wouldn't matter whether you asked a minister, a counselor, or the man on the street; their answers would vary according to the knowledge, character, and experiences of each person you asked. May this poor student offer his humble opinion once more? Allow me to go back to what the Lord Jesus said…what God therefore hath joined together, let not man put asunder. When the union of two persons is accompanied by the presence of the Holy Spirit, that union will be far stronger than a union which was not accompanied by the Holy Spirit. It is there – right there, at that critical juncture; the point at which the union is made – the joining of two persons together as one, that the Marriage is the most vulnerable. Everything which comes after the joining of the two is affected by the union itself. The success or failure of the joining of two rails ultimately determines the success or failure of the whole track. And so it is in a Marriage ceremony. The joining of the two, as far as I am concerned, is the most important moment in the Marriage. But I reserve the right to be wrong, and I heartily welcome any and all reasonable argument to the contrary.

Who among us is able, with any degree of certainty, to determine which part of the railroad is the most important? Is it the bed of gravel into which the heavy crossties are tamped securely? Are the crossties themselves more important than the bed beneath them? And what of the steel plates upon which the rail rests? How important is the rail itself? And of what value would any of the aforementioned pieces be if not for the heavy spikes that hold the steel plate to the wood, and the steel rail to the plate? Surely we can see the value, nay, the necessity of each of the parts that make up the whole. Take away any one of these components, and you are left with a dysfunctional apparatus which is both useless and dangerous. The Marriage, like the railroad, must have all its proper components in their proper places in order to function properly.

The spikes cannot do the job of the bolts; the bolts cannot function without the nuts; the nuts and bolts are useless without the steel plate; none of these can take the place of the rail itself; and all of these are joined together, side by side, near the ends of the heavy crossties, embedded deeply into the bed of gravel. But the minister in me must, because of the very nature of my calling, make a point about the wood, the plates, and the spikes. These three things hold everything else together. Without them, the whole thing would fall apart. No man in his right mind would attempt to run a train upon a set of tracks with no steel plates, no crossties, and no spikes. And I am almost certain that the reader, if he or she has read the Bible, and knows the old old story of Jesus and His Cross, can see where the writer is going with this. Let us make His hands the "plates", through which the "spikes" were driven into the wood of the Cross. And then let us ask the question – Is this not what holds everything together? His hands, outstretched as far as his tormentors could pull them, each at one end of the Cross, pierced by the cruel spikes, pinning Him to the wood – this, more than anything else, is what holds Marriages, homes, families, churches, communities and countries together. And without this, it all falls apart, and becomes a thing at which others mock, wondering why it failed, and wondering how and why so many were affected as a result of its failure.

It is not mere coincidence that whenever a Marriage, a business, or any other entity involving more than one person turns out to be a disaster, often causing severe damage to both persons and property, the failure and the fallout are called *"a train wreck"*. I have heard many ministers, after having performed a wedding ceremony, watching the couple as they walked away, make the comment – *"There goes a train wreck waiting to happen."* I have often wanted to ask those ministers why they performed the ceremony with those sentiments in their own hearts. Train wrecks do not just happen without a cause. Most train wrecks, when investigated, turn out to be the result of human error. And so it is with Marriages. Some train wrecks are, of course, attributed to "mechanical failure" or "equipment failure" of some kind. But none of the persons involved in the process of joining two persons in matrimony can blame the failure of a Marriage on *"mechanical failure."* When a marriage fails, it may take a while to trace the cause of the failure back to the source of the failure, but when the source is discovered, it turns out that one or more humans were involved.

As I near the end of this chapter, I feel it needful to remind the reader that in a railroad system, there are inspectors, each assigned to a certain section of the railroad in a particular locale. It is his or her job to carefully inspect each part of the track, looking for faulty or worn out components that may be, or become hazardous to the operation of the system. If he or she finds something amiss, it must be reported as soon as possible so the problem can be fixed before a disaster happens. Judy Jordan, a retired railroad Yard Master, who has collaborated closely with me in writing this book, has furnished invaluable information concerning the inspecting and maintenance of railroad tracks. Judy tells me that every part of the railroad track, including the bed of gravel, is regularly inspected, both internally and externally, looking for any kind of defect, whether great or small. She also informed me that with the ever changing weather conditions that affect every part of the system, additional inspections are required to ensure the system is safe for everyone concerned. And here is where the comparison between a railroad and a Marriage breaks down. The operational parts of a railroad are inspected frequently and carefully. An impending disaster can be averted by ongoing inspections.

In a Marriage, however, there is no designated *"inspector"* who carefully and regularly inspects the operation, unless the husband and wife themselves are vigilant, and ever watching for telltale signs of deterioration in any area of the Marriage. It has been my experience in counseling couples that most married individuals never take the time to stand back and take a long look at their relationship. And most couples definitely do not want anyone else *"inspecting"* their relationship for them. The railroad inspector is a compensated employee of the railroad. He gets paid to inspect the track, and receives additional benefits other than his paycheck to give him or her further incentive to do the best job possible in maintaining high standards of safety for all those involved in the operation of the railroad, and for the safety of the public.

I have said that the Marriage has no *"**designated inspector**"* who regularly and carefully monitors all the component parts that make up a Marriage relationship. Please allow me to clarify that statement a bit. Once a Marriage has taken place, regardless of how well or how poorly that Marriage performs, there is one Inspector, who is not of this world, who monitors every single moment, every word, and every action that takes place in that Marriage. God Himself, the One who instituted Marriage, has inspected every Marriage that has ever taken place since the Marriage of Adam and Eve, and He will inspect every Marriage that takes place from this moment forward. I must strongly disagree with some of my peers, who insist that God does not see what goes on behind the closed doors of the Marriage bedroom. Some of these same folks insist that God doesn't even care about what happens in the Marriage bedroom. I believe this next chapter, entitled *"**Intimacy**"*, will prove otherwise.

Chapter Five

The "i" in Marriage = Intimacy

Many years ago I was asked to write a brief, contracted paper on the subject of intimacy. My greatest difficulty in writing that paper was the limitation the professor imposed upon me to – **keep it short.** If I may employ the old axiom – *"the shortest distance between two points is a straight line",* and if I may quote Shakespeare's character, Polonius, – *"since brevity is the soul of wit, I will be brief",* here goes. **Intimacy is as far above sex as Heaven is above the Earth** – Chapter Six.

No, just kidding! But the rest of this chapter could be summed up in the sentence above. The problem that exists in recognizing the immeasurable difference between ***intimacy*** and ***sex*** is that most humans (if any,) have never experienced intimacy. Few humans know its definition. And at the risk of being mocked, ridiculed, or even disowned by some of my colleagues, I must follow the inclinations of my conscience here. With only the slightest reservation, I must say that I am doubtful that any two humans, including Adam and Eve, have experienced pure, unadulterated intimacy. In the same way a great number of persons do not recognize the difference between love and lust, neither have they known the astronomical distance which separates intimacy from that dirty thing the world has come to call sex. In fact, in nearly every culture on planet Earth, no difference at all is recognized between sex and intimacy – for they are one and the same in most (if not all) cultures. Even my dictionary defines intimacy as sex. Sorry Mr. Webster, but I must respectfully disagree with you.

Without a moment's hesitation, and with no degree of reservation, let the author go on record saying – there can be sex without intimacy, and if we define our terms correctly, there can be intimacy without sex. In its original setting, Marriage consisted of intimacy as a ***presupposition***, with sex as a ***privilege*** stemming from that presupposition. God designed intimacy between a man and wife to produce offspring. The ***privilege*** of the physical act of sex between them was no more than God's grace, granting both the man and the woman the most superlative ecstasy two humans can experience within that sacred realm of intimacy.

The whole problem of differentiating between the two terms – intimacy and sex, is that both were affected by the Fall of Adam, so that neither term now has the same definition as the original term. In order to understand intimacy in its original setting, we must include the physical act of sex, but we must define the act of sex – ***as it would have been*** - before ***sin happened***. When Adam and Eve were created they were naked – and they were not ashamed of their nakedness to any degree. It was God's intention for the man and the woman to engage in intimacy, with the natural result of producing offspring. Can we imagine an intimacy untainted by sin, in which two perfectly created beings could engage without any degree of shame? If Adam and Eve were not ashamed of their ***nakedness*** before the Fall, neither would they have been ashamed of their ***intimacy***, which would have involved the physical act of sexual intercourse. Our fallen nature renders us incapable of even imagining the height of ecstasy to which the couple would have risen in the act of intimacy – had they not sinned. But sin has entered, and has blighted, stained and sullied the most beautiful thing which God gave to the man and the woman. Intimacy, as it was intended to be, has never been experienced by any two human beings, not even Adam and Eve. Their first act of sexual intercourse happened ***after they had sinned***, and was therefore necessarily less than what it could, and should have been, if they had not sinned.

Again the writer has hesitated. The paragraph below this one was written first, then the writer had to pause, pray, and come back and insert this paragraph between the one above it and the one below it. In the paragraph above I intimated that no two human beings have experienced intimacy as God originally intended it. I stand by that statement, and offer no apology for it. But with all reverence, I must add that there ***may have been*** one person who did, one time only, experience that intimacy, that person being, of course, the Virgin Mary in the conception of Jesus Christ by the Holy Ghost. But I promise I will not go on the defensive or be angry or offended if anyone wishes to offer a rational contradiction. Please do not misread what the writer has written – I must strongly emphasize the –"***may have***", on Mary's part, simply because, contrary to the belief, the dogma, of my Catholic friends, this writer does not believe in The Immaculate Conception of Mary. I do believe in the Immaculate Conception of Jesus Christ, and Him only. I cannot accept that there has ever been another human being, other than Christ, who was conceived without the taint of original sin.

Now that sin has done its terrible work upon man and all his faculties, the closest thing to intimacy, as God intended it, which fallen men can experience in the physical realm is that of two persons, a man and a woman, united in holy matrimony, accompanied by the Holy Spirit, engaging in the act of sexual intercourse. And will the reader agree that there is absolutely no experience *in the spiritual realm* greater, higher, or more fulfilling than the *spiritual intimacy* between God and His people? And what is the design – the intent of this spiritual intimacy? Is it not that there should be offspring produced? Even in his fallen state, man has been given the privilege of engaging in the most fulfilling and gratifying experience which the fallen flesh can know. And should it not make us look upward with grateful hearts, knowing that our God foreknew our needs, and provided for all of them? How much more, then, should we long for that *most gratifying of all spiritual experiences* – the power and presence of He the Holy Spirit in our souls!

 With the Fall of Adam, and the ensuing depravity which now affects every faculty of the entire race, there is nothing in all of creation that can be enjoyed or appreciated in the same way it was enjoyed and appreciated before Adam's fall, not only because of the depravity of the race, but also because creation itself is now corrupted. There is nothing in the Universe today which bears the same pristine beauty with which it was created originally. All of creation bears the marks of the curse God pronounced in the Garden.

All realms and all relationships are now less than what they were originally, including the relationship between man and wife. In our bodies of flesh, we are incapable of knowing or feeling what Adam and Eve knew and felt before they sinned. Whatever treasures or pleasures we do enjoy, that enjoyment is somewhat less than what it could have been had our first parents simply obeyed the words of their Creator.

And it gets worse from there! Not only is all of creation corrupted, groaning and travailing under the curse, but fallen men seem bent upon corrupting it even further. And the most precious and sacred relationship which God made – Marriage, is no exception. Men of corrupt minds are not content to leave well enough alone. They must go to the utmost length, breadth, depth and height of moral corruption which their depraved and demented minds can imagine. If intimacy could be defined with any degree of certitude by fallen men, fallen men will eventually find *another way to define it*, and after *re-defining* it, they will then *follow* what they believe to be right and proper practices, all of which are based upon their *new definition* of the term. This is how men justify their thoughts and actions – by re-defining those sacred terms which were once held sacred. But the saddest part of the whole sordid mess is that these same men (and women) have the audacity to use (I should say misuse,) the very Word of God in an attempt to justify their thoughts and actions – and especially in the bedroom!

The verse I used at the beginning of this book is only one of many which millions of individuals and couples have latched onto as justification for whatever they wish to do in the bedroom. But in the same way many other verses and passages of Scripture are misinterpreted, misused, and misapplied, so it is with this verse. Those whose hearts insist upon having their own way, more often than not, take only part of a verse, and leave off the rest of it, and come away with what they believe to be the perfect answer to their perverted desires and urges. Please look closely at the verse again:

Marriage is honorable in all, and the bed undefiled: but whoremongers and adulterers God will judge (Hebrews 13:4 KJV).

If I had a dollar for every time I've had **the first nine words** of that verse quoted to me, I could have retired from the trucking industry much sooner than I did. In fact, most individuals (mostly men) who come to me for advice and/or counseling only employ **three words from the verse,** because those are the only three words in the entire verse they remember. And the reason they only remember those three words is – they don't see the rest of the verse, **because they**

don't want to see the rest of the verse. Those three words, of course, are…*the bed undefiled*. I am not exaggerating when I say that 95% of all men who have sat across my desk from me are able to quote those three words, but cannot quote another single word from that verse. Why? Because those are the three words which, according to modern ideology, allow anything and everything, and prohibit nothing that happens in the marriage bedroom. Allow the author to illustrate from real life the truth of what he has just written.

Many years ago, when a certain Pastor and his wife were in their early thirties, the Pastor happened to overhear a conversation which he was not supposed to hear. In the basement of the church, the Sunday School rooms were partitioned off by thin room dividers. The class the Pastor was teaching and the class another teacher was teaching were separated by less than half an inch of un-insulated partition; the Pastor could hear every word the other teacher was saying. The other teacher was unaware that the Pastor was on the other side of the partition. Thankfully, the Pastor's wife wasn't in either of the classes that Sunday, because she was teaching another class further down the hall. He thanked God also that there was only one other person – a man, in his class at the moment. He also heard every word. The other class consisted of young men and women in their early twenties. The conversation the Pastor and his class heard had absolutely nothing to do with the Sunday School lesson the teacher was supposed to be teaching. And to make matters worse, the wife of the other teacher was in his class, hearing everything that was said. Here is part of what the other gentleman and the Pastor heard:

Teacher: *"You know, I bet our Pastor and his wife are both wildcats in the bedroom."* After a few loud laughs and *"amens"*, the teacher's wife responded:

"Well, you're probably right, but whatever they do behind closed doors in the privacy of their home is perfectly alright, and it's nobody else's business, because the Bible says God doesn't look into the bedroom, and the marriage bed is undefiled."

The Pastor had heard enough. He pushed back the partition between them, confronted the teacher and his wife, and asked them to leave the church immediately. The two of them have not spoken to the Pastor from that day to this. But the point is this – not only did the teacher's wife misquote the Scriptures, and add to the Scriptures, she also misinterpreted the part she did quote correctly. But again, the thing which struck the Pastor's heart like a poisoned dart was the fact that those young men and women not only heard the sordid insinuation, but they were agreeing with it. I have no way of knowing the present mentality or morality of the person reading this chapter right now, but if the reader has come this far, and hasn't discarded the book, I pray that he or she can at least continue reading to the end of this chapter. There may be, no, there are those who relish the idea of being compared to animals when it comes to their so called "***sex life***". I am not one of them, and neither is my beloved wife. And may God help the man and woman whose marriage has reached a state of decadence that requires animalistic behavior in the bedroom in order for the marriage to survive. In all honesty, it is my humble opinion that marriage has already failed, and is probably beyond repair, unless God Himself takes command of it.

I fully understand that there are millions of folks who are going to disagree with some, if not all of what I write in this book. And one of the many arguments which so many use against my position on the subject of intimacy is that old expedient – *"the Bible is open to interpretation."* Those who use this expedient, of course, use it to their own advantage, granting themselves a license to practice whatever their hearts desire to practice without any shame. These same folks demand that I, and those who see things the same way I see them, give them the liberty and license to interpret the Scriptures in their favor. And their interpretation of those three words – (the bed undefiled,) is that no matter what they do upon that bed, the bed remains undefiled. But these same folks adamantly deny me the license to interpret those same words a different way. I will be the first to agree that the marriage bed is undefiled, but only for as long as those who sleep on it keep it undefiled.

It is so easy for men (and women,) both Christian and non-Christian, to take three simple words from the Bible, and interpret those words in such a way that those words give them an open-ended avenue of self indulgence in which they can engage with no shame, using the words of God as justification for their sordid, sensual, and sometimes sadistic behavior. I took the liberty of entitling this chapter *"intimacy"* for more than one reason. First of all, there is probably no other term that would fit the letter *"i"* in Marriage better than intimacy. And secondly, it was the desire of my heart to honor my Lord and His Word throughout this book. And since the terms *intimacy* and *sex* are not mentioned in the Bible, it is a bit difficult to fully define, describe, or elaborate on them to everyone's satisfaction, including my own. The one term in the Bible which, I believe, best defines the modern term ***"sex"*** is the Hebrew word *"**yada**"*, which the translators translated into English as ***"know"***. And the phrase which, I believe, best describes the act of sexual intercourse is…*to lie with*, meaning, of course, to lie down together with the intent of having a sexual relationship. But when it comes to the term "*intimacy*", this poor student can find no other term in the Bible which defines or describes it better than - **Love.** And in the same way perverted men have altered the definitions of all the other sacred terms which apply to Marriage, the term, Love, is no exception. And this writer can think of no other entity in the world that has polluted and disgraced that term more than a certain entity in a place called Hollywood, California, USA.

The beloved Apostle Paul, in the thirteenth chapter of his first letter to the Corinthians, lists several things which…*love does not do.* In verses five and six of that chapter, we are given four things which love does not do, and two things love does do. Three of those things which love does not do have to do with sexual activities between men and women. And does the writer even have to remind anyone that all sexual activity is to be limited to persons who are legally married to each other? The first thing mentioned in verse five which love does not do is…*it does not behave itself unseemly.* The term "*unseemly*" almost defines itself, but in case anyone who reads this book may need a little extra help in understanding it, it means (a) indecent, (b) unbecoming, (c) not seemly, (d) not proper. And since the writer has committed himself to this task unreservedly, with God's honor and glory in mind, he must go beyond the dictionary, and add another definition to the term "unseemly", namely, (e) immoral. May God and Mr. Webster forgive me if I am in error in defining that which is unseemly as that which is immoral.

I ask, is it seemly, proper, becoming, moral, or decent for two human beings created in the image of God to abandon their God-given humanity, even temporarily, for the sake of a few moments or hours of pretending to be animals? That is not love, that is not intimacy, and that is not even sex in its proper context; it is ***bestiality in disguise, masquerading as humanity, and calling itself intimacy.*** What decent man, helplessly in love with his wife, will subject her to such bestial behavior? And what decent woman would allow it? The mentality of those who promote and practice animalistic behavior in the bedroom is that – because it is done behind closed doors, between two consenting adults, it is therefore justified, and nothing in which their hearts and bodies wish to engage is off limits to them. In other words, the location is the justification. But then they go a step farther, invoking the ***imagined justification*** which they believe is given to them by those three words in Hebrews 13:4 – ***the bed undefiled***. But the thing of which these folks are either willfully or un-willfully ignorant is that the term – ***bed***, in the context in which it is used in this verse, does not mean simply the bed itself. The Marriage bed includes the bed, and everything that happens on that bed, verbally, physically, and morally.

But the saddest and most heart-wrenching thing of all is that this immoral mentality has made its way into the churches, from the pulpit to the pew. Many ministers, fearful of losing some of their members, have acquiesced, condescended, and conformed to this mentality and all the sordid practices which proceed from it, using these same three words from Hebrews 13:4 as their justification. I do not like to repeat hear-say evidence, so let me put this in the form of a question – What decent minister would tolerate, let alone encourage those to whom he ministers to go and watch a movie which portrays the most sordid and sadistic acts in which two human beings can engage? And what God-fearing, Bible-believing man or woman would want to go and see the filth in the first place? A few comments which this Pastor has heard firsthand from some folks who attend church regularly include – 1. *"Seeing this movie has greatly enhanced our sex life, and may have even saved our marriage."* And another insinuation, directed at myself, from a married couple from another church – 2. *"Pastor, you really should go and see this movie. We believe it might change your perspective on marital intimacy."* 3. *"Pastor, if you will go and see this movie, it will better equip you to minister to those whose marriages are experiencing sexual problems."*

These are only a few of the many comments this Pastor has heard from folks who were seemingly the most godly and dedicated Christians he had ever known, until a certain movie came out of Hollywood. It is not very difficult for me to understand how unbelievers might get caught up in the sordid hysteria that surrounds these so-called *blockbuster* films, but I cannot understand how Christians - we who are supposed to hold ourselves to a higher standard than that of the unbeliever, can lower our standards to a level similar to that of the brute beast, and justify it all behind a closed door, quoting three words from the Bible as the basis of our less-than-human behavior. And if all this writer has written so far has not to any degree differentiated between that which is sacred (intimacy) and that which is vile (sexual perversion), then it is doubtful that anything else he may write will convince anyone of the immeasurable distance between the two. And yet he must keep writing, because the very nature of that sacred term – **intimacy,** deserves and demands every ounce of his God-given strength in an attempt to show how far God has separated the precious from the vile. And that brings up the next thing which love does not do – **love seeketh not her own.**

One of the most difficult things a Pastor or counselor ever has to do is to get the whole truth from those who come to him for counseling. Not many men or women are quite ready or willing to disclose the darker secrets of their hearts to another person without holding some little something back from him. And this reluctance or outright refusal to "*come clean*" necessarily limits the Pastor or counselor as to how much he or she can do for the person or persons receiving the counseling. But the Pastor or counselor, in spite of the limited information he is given, must do everything in his power to reach "*the heart of the matter*", without offending those on the other side of his desk, if that is at all possible. And here I must again reach way back to my younger days as a Pastor and counselor, and bring out one of the old, but highly effective counseling methods of some of those wise old men who mentored me years ago. Quoting from a very wise and very experienced Pastor of yesteryear, he said to me – "*Son, when you're trying to pry the lid off another man's love life, start with a pen knife. If the pen knife doesn't work, use a screwdriver. If the screwdriver doesn't work, try a bigger screwdriver. And if the bigger screwdriver doesn't* work, *you have only one other option."* I waited patiently for the elder Pastor's last resort, as with a big smile, he added – *"use a crowbar."*

I fully understood the good Pastor's metaphors. When folks come to you for marriage counseling, you cannot assume anything. You do not immediately begin to ask questions about the couple's sex life. You sit and listen, and you take notes - mental notes if you have a good memory, and scribbled notes if you do not. You listen and you learn. You do not jump to conclusions, you wait for confessions. If the couple is sincerely seeking help, they will eventually give you bits of truth upon which you can build. Instead of jumping to a **conclusion,** allow the couple to create their own **preclusion.** In other words, trap them with their own truth. Once a truth has been established, that truth precludes, it forbids them from going back and lying to you. That is the pen knife. But using a pen knife to pry open a lid that is nailed securely takes a lot of time and effort, and may even break the pen knife if not used carefully and slowly. It may even fail utterly to get at any truth at all. Now it's time for the screwdriver.

You begin to ask questions. Your discerning spirit tells you they have told you some truth, but not all the truth.

You begin prying at one corner of the lid, ever so gently. I am confident the reader is now able to discern where the writer is going with this, so let's save some time and perhaps a tree or two, and get to the point. You tried the pen knife, the screwdriver, and the bigger screwdriver, and yet the most important truth lies hidden from you. Your last option is the crowbar. I have never met a wooden lid yet that can resist the power and leverage of a steel crowbar. Here you must insist that if you are to help the couple, they must come clean, and tell you all the truth, because that is one of the things love does – it rejoices in the truth (v.6b).

How many men or women do you know who will quickly confess that the only person they want to please in the bedroom is himself, or herself? How many will admit that the things they have done in the bedroom are unseemly? And there it is – "***the heart of the matter***", the cold hard truth which so many, nay, too many are unwilling to face. The couple does not have a "*sexual problem*", they have an "***intimacy problem***", they have a "*love problem*". If love seeks not her own things, then whose things does she seek? She seeks the things, the satisfaction, the joy, the fulfillment, the ecstasy of the other person. The joy, the satisfaction, the fulfillment, and the ecstasy of the other person are, in themselves, the joy, satisfaction, fulfillment and ecstasy of the one seeking them for the other. That is **human intimacy** at its most sacred height. The one lives for the other, with the other, and vicariously through the other. And that is what it means to become one flesh – one feels what the other feels by each giving themselves completely to the other, seeking – not his own good, but the good of the other.

And lest anyone should misread the intent of the author here, let me establish every word as solidly as I possibly can. I am not in any way, or to any degree, limiting human intimacy to the physical act of sexual intercourse. If love seeks not her own things, she does not seek her own things (satisfaction, joy, fulfillment, etc.) even from something as simple and innocent as a kiss. I can never forget the first time I kissed the young lady who is now my wife of 49 years. We were both fifteen at the time. It was on Easter Sunday, 1966, around 2:00 p.m. It happened a few yards down the dirt road from her house, standing beside a white 1958 Chevrolet, which belonged to her older brother. My heart was pounding like a pneumatic jackhammer. It was I who took the initiative, pulling her close to me, looking deeply into her blue eyes, wondering if I should kiss her, or get in the car and drive away. Her eyes told me it was ok to kiss her, and did I ever kiss her! I put every ounce of passion in my soul into that kiss. It must have been the proper thing to do, because we have now been married 49 years. We have three children, seven grandchildren, and one great granddaughter. The passion I put into that first kiss was not for my own gratification – it was for hers. I had to try to make her feel what I was feeling for her. She responded in kind, kissing me with all the passion in her soul. We courted for two years, and in that two years, we did a lot of kissing. In 49 years of marriage, she has known that I live for her, and not for myself, and I know that she lives for me, not for herself, because love seeks not her own things, but the things of others.

When I asked my dear wife for her input in writing this book, I didn't ask for any specific opinion or stance upon any particular aspect of marriage. I wanted her honest and spontaneous response, without any consideration for how I might react to it. She responded without hesitation. She said – ***"Tell them that making love begins as soon as the two of you wake up, and continues throughout the day, and it only gets better when the lights go out."***

And yet another thing which *love does not do*, not even behind closed doors - love *thinketh no evil*. Is there evil in the marriage bedroom? And if there is, from whence did it spring? It sprang from the thoughts of one or both participants, and the thoughts evolved into actions. If we are not well-acquainted with the Scriptures, and know little or nothing about the rules of Scriptural exegesis (interpretation), we are likely, if not certain, to misinterpret the kind of love the Apostle describes in these two verses – 5&6. How can fallen men and women, born in sin, and conceived in iniquity, possess a love that disallows an evil thought? We can try to rely upon our own understanding and rationalizations, or we can trust the Holy Spirit to help us understand it. If, as the Bible teaches…all have sinned, and come short of the glory of God, (Romans 3:23), then there has never been a human being other than Jesus Christ who has not had an evil thought, spoken an evil word, or done an evil deed. And is there a kind of love which is able to preclude, forbid, or disallow any evil thought from invading the human mind? This, of course, is a rhetorical question – it answers itself.

How, then, are we to understand Paul's teaching? Perhaps a little illustration from another preacher from the past may help. Dr. Martin Luther King Sr., when questioned about the thoughts and actions of men and women, said – *"I may not be able to prevent a bird from landing on my head, but I can prevent him from building his nest there."* Dr. King, of course, was referring to all fallen men, and their inability to prevent evil thoughts from crossing their minds.

But they are capable of preventing those thoughts from evolving into actions. But according to Paul, inspired by the Holy Spirit, there must yet be a kind of love (intimacy,) which is able to enable fallen men, at least for a time, to experience the absence of evil thoughts. But when, where, and how can this experience be known? I dare say that 90% or more of humanity worldwide would quickly agree that the bedroom would be the last place where no evil thought would occur. May I humbly submit to you that in my opinion and experience, that is exactly the place and time wherein no evil thought should invade the heart, mind, and spirit of either the man or woman. And if an evil thought does occur in that bedroom that, in itself, confirms Paul's teaching. If love thinks no evil, then the presence of evil proves that the kind of love Paul is describing is not there – it is absent.

And finally, in verse six of I Corinthians, chapter thirteen, we have the last thing that love does not do – **love rejoiceth not in iniquity**. I have often wondered how men and women who are highly intelligent and very gifted in many areas, can read the Holy Bible, and yet come away with an attitude which clearly shows their lack of respect for that Book. When I read the words – *"love does not rejoice in iniquity"*, not only do I ponder the meaning of the statement, but if I am the Christian that I profess to be, I must bind myself to that statement, I must submit to that statement, and I must practice the precept taught in that statement.

The hearts of men and women are laid bare in so many ways. The places we go, the events in which we participate, the ideals we promote, and the people with whom we associate, all reveal another little piece of our character. The things of which we approve, the things and persons we applaud, the things we choose as entertainment, and the things in which we rejoice, these also tell us, and others, where our hearts are the most satisfied. Show me the man, young or old, who pollutes his mind with pornography in any of its sordid forms, and I'll show you a man who *rejoices in iniquity.* I am often asked by those I serve if I have seen this movie or that movie, or if I watched the awards ceremony where actors and actresses are awarded and applauded for their portrayals of adultery, fornication, incest, sodomy, and every other sordid sexual perversity which producers, directors and actors are capable of producing. My answer is always the same – No, I haven't watched the movie, and No, I haven't watched the awards ceremony.

I am often reminded by those who watch these affairs that the actors and actresses who portray these characters and their sadistic behavior are only acting, pretending, and not really doing anything wrong or sinful. I must respectfully disagree. But I will not spend a lot of time here defending my position on that point. If the reader will read my other book – Giving The Devil his Due, he or she will see clearly where this Pastor stands on the issue of smut, in all of its forms, pretended or otherwise.

The intimacy of which I have been writing is far too sacred for me to leave out anything that might help toward causing the reader to see the stark contrast between it and that sickening, sensual, sordid, sadistic thing which most of the world has come to know as "sex". And in the same way the devil and his demons love to mask that which is ugly and filthy, and dress it up in more appealing garments to make it appear acceptable, he changes, not only the definition of the terms, but the terminology associated with them. Sex, as it is defined and practiced by so many millions, is often referred to as *"making love"*. And when those who expose their nakedness, and pretend to *"make love"* on the big screen, those who watch, not only watch, but approve and applaud the filth, which is the same thing as …rejoicing in iniquity, and love does not rejoice in iniquity. A Christian has no business, and definitely no incentive to pollute his or her mind with the foul, fiendish filth that pours out of the minds and mouths of those who promote, produce, and practice it.

And neither does the Christian have any business approving, applauding, or rejoicing in any of it.

Chapter Six

The second "a" in Marriage = Alternatives

Whenever men and women are not happy, content, or accepting of anything which seems to impose any degree of restriction upon them in any way, they have two choices – they can either come to accept the restriction and abide by it, or they can come up with an alternative of their own making, which is to their own liking, and simply ignore, neglect, or rise up against the law, rule, or ordinance which restricts them from doing what they want to do. And in forty plus years of ministry, I can think of no other object, law, or belief system against which mankind has kicked as violently as he has against the Holy Bible. The Holy Bible is a Divine Book, containing laws and precepts which are binding upon every human being who has ever existed, or who will ever exist in the future. I realize that is a broad statement, and millions of persons from ever race, color, creed and tongue may immediately call me a bigot and/or a fool if they read these words. Nevertheless, I stand by the statement without any degree of reservation or shame.

There is no other inspired book, period. If there is another inspired book in the world, that would make the Christian Bible a lie, and its Author a liar, and neither of these is possible. If there is another inspired book somewhere in the Universe, then Christianity is a false religion, with no salvation and no Savior. In all my years of study, travel, and my walk with Christ, I have heard some folks claim they have a book that is equally inspired as the Holy Bible, but that cannot be, because every other book which lays claim to any degree of divine inspiration, somewhere in its pages, contradicts the Holy Bible. And if the reader is now thinking that the writer is digressing from his point, please be patient with the writer for a few more moments.

Those who do not like or accept the teaching of the Holy Bible on the subject of Marriage, or any other subject for that matter, have a choice to make. By rejecting the teaching of Scripture, they must necessarily find an alternative to the teaching of the Bible – an alternative which suits their own fancy, and satisfies their own concept of what Marriage means. And since there is no other inspired book by which they can define what a true Marriage is, they are left with a counterfeit plan – something which looks a lot like Marriage, sounds a lot like Marriage, and to a large degree, satisfies the lusts and longings of the flesh for a while. This is what fallen men want, a relationship in which they make their own rules, set their own standards, and practice their own precepts. And in order to have this kind of relationship, they must first discard the Holy Bible. And when the counterfeit concept begins to fail them; when the burning flames of lust die down into a glowing ember; when whatever it was that first attracted them to each other has now become a faint memory, and they must invent new ways of keeping each other interested, the cold hard truth stares them in the face – they are not in love with each other at all – it was all just a high degree of physical attraction, mixed with heightened emotions which ebb and flow like the tides. They consult a marriage counselor who tells them they need to re-kindle the flame of their love for each other, going backward in time to that time and place where they supposedly *"fell in love"*.

Neither of them is willing to admit that what they feel for each other is not real love, and so, in order to convince their mate that it is real love, he or she (or both) must pretend, both inside and outside the bedroom. The marriage has already failed, and unless God intervenes, and unless His Word becomes the textbook, and the standard by which they begin to live, they are doomed to a life of misery, shame, and pretense. They may call their sexual relationship by whatever term or terms they choose, but it is not love, it is not intimacy – it is an alternative with which they pretend to be happy. This, of course, is only one of many alternative means by which untold numbers of couples maintain an appearance of having a *"**good**"* marriage. Some of these relationships continue for years, or even a lifetime, never having known the meaning of true intimacy, to whatever degree intimacy can be experienced by fallen humanity.

Another alternative to the kind of Marriage defined and described in the Holy Scriptures is what I would call – **the Hollywood marriage.** But lest I should also offend the few godly persons who inhabit that realm, I will rather call it the **"*arrangement*".** And I must quickly differentiate between an **"*arranged*"** marriage, as practiced in many eastern cultures, and elsewhere, and a marriage which is no more than an "*arrangement*", with all the details worked out in advance, including a prenuptial agreement, scrutinized by both parties and their attorneys. It is an arrangement wherein one or both parties are so wealthy, they agree that, should the marriage end in divorce, each party retains most, if not all, of his or her estate. I have neither the time nor the patience to go into all the little details which are negotiated into some of these agreements, but suffice it to say that in some of these arrangements, both parties even agree upon how many times they are to engage in whatever it is they call *"lovemaking"* each week. In some other of these "arrangements", it is agreed beforehand that – "if this doesn't work out, we can always get a divorce." And then there are other marriages which allow either the husband or wife, or both, to engage in sexual activities with the wives and husbands of other married couples, including the men with the men, the women with the women, or the husband with the other man's wife, or the wife with the other woman's husband, or all of these. They call themselves *"swingers"*.

Yet another alternative to Marriage which men and women have so easily and expediently accepted is that of **cohabitating**; living together, shacking up, without a license. And here again, the author must tread carefully, reverently, and with compassion. Some of the most godly people I know today, after having fallen into this trap, and having lived together for any number of years, have realized that what they were doing was wrong, and have since made a commitment to God and each other, gotten married, and now live happy and productive lives. And what, you may ask, made the difference? And I answer - God and His Word made the difference. When folks come to know the Lord

Jesus Christ personally, He makes a radical difference in their perspective on virtually every aspect of human existence, including the sacred realm of Marriage. I must again steer the reader away from this book and into the inspired Word of God, where, if I have understood correctly, we are taught that – if a young man and woman have engaged in pre-marital sex, and later realize they have sinned, and then get married, it is the same as if they had not sinned, but…What saith the Scripture? The Apostle Paul again gives us exactly what we need to understand the compassionate and forgiving heart of God. In I Corinthians 7:35&36, we read:

And this I speak for your own profit; not that I may cast a snare upon you, but for that which is comely, and that ye may attend upon the Lord without distraction. But if any man think that he behaveth himself uncomely toward his virgin, if she pass the flower of her age, and need so require, let him do what he will, he sinneth not: let them marry.

What has happened in verse 36? A young man has behaved uncomely toward his espoused virgin. She has passed the age of puberty. He has decided he can't wait until after the wedding ceremony to engage in sexual intercourse with her. He has a need which he is either incapable or unwilling to deny. So he has sex with her. Now what? There is only one option – he must marry her. And when he marries her, the sin he committed before the ceremony is negated, nullified, in the eyes of God. But what if he does not marry her? Then His sin remains, un-forgiven. But the main point, and what I believe to be the clear teaching of these verses is that, **they are to be married, either way**. I ask you, which scenario would you prefer for your son or daughter – (a) a sexual relationship outside of marriage, with no marriage later; (b) a sexual relationship outside of marriage with a marriage later, or (c) two virgins marrying without a sexual relationship beforehand? Yeah, that's what I thought you'd say! The fact that virtually every culture that has existed since the dawn of humanity, whether Christian or non-Christian, prefers that their children remain pure before marriage, is, in itself, the proof, the validation that sexual purity before marriage is the best way. And it is the best way because it is God's way, as taught in God's Word. Unfortunately, far too many young men, and women, have used these verses as justification for engaging in premarital sex. But let this Pastor be as plain as God and His Word allow – there is no justification, or permission of premarital sex anywhere in the Holy Bible. Yes, God has made allowances for the sinfulness of men, and given them the means by which they may make amends for their errors in judgment, but let no man or woman take these allowances to mean that God, in any way, or to any degree, approves or condones these actions.

The teaching of this little book, or any other book which has anything to say about morality, will either stand or fall to the extent that it either agrees or disagrees with the Word of God. As long as it agrees with the Word, it will stand, and be a blessing to all who read it. But the moment at which it disagrees with, or contradicts the Word of God, it will fall, and great will be the fall of it. Of the books that I have written, or had a part in writing, this one, and one other, (Giving the Devil His Due,) have been the most difficult and time-consuming. It is not an easy task to put on paper that which is in the heart, if the writer fears God, and wishes to honor Him with every statement. He must choose his words carefully, and prayerfully, lest he dishonor the greatest Book of all, and its Author. He must have a working knowledge of the Bible as a whole, and God-given wisdom in the understanding of all its parts. And while he must be careful not to deliberately offend either Jew, Gentile, or the church of God, he must also hate evil in all of its forms, because the writer of Psalm 97, in verse ten, wrote:

Ye that love the Lord, hate evil.

We are not to hate the evildoer, but we must hate the evil itself, if we love God. We are not to vent our hatred of evil upon those who commit it, but we are to pray for them, love them, be kind to them, and show them a better way. And this brings me to my closing example of what happens when men call bitter sweet, and sweet bitter; when they call light darkness, and darkness light; when they call good evil and evil good; when men and women choose an alternative means, method or motive other than that which God has prescribed in His Word.

This last alternative to Marriage, of which millions of men and women have approved, which millions have applauded and adopted, is the one which has become so widely accepted in so many cultures, many Christians and Christian ministers seem reluctant, and some even refuse, to confront it head on. And like so many other evils that have crept into the churches, this also has made its way into the pulpit and the pew. *Same-sex marriage*, terms which ought not to be mentioned together in the same breath, has become the scourge of humanity, and yet is accepted as an alternate life style by those who propose, promote and practice it. Here and now, I throw down the gauntlet, challenging any man, woman, child, or any group of men, women or children, or any mixture thereof, to show a single instance anywhere in the Holy Bible where it is even remotely or vaguely insinuated that a man married another man, or that a woman married another woman.

    The glaring absence of such an insinuation in the Holy Bible is the only incentive I need to speak out against the practice of it. Nay, I must go farther – I must condemn the putrid, poisonous practice for what it is. It is sinful, it is abominable, it is unnatural, it is a slap in the face of a Holy God, and a denial of the veracity of His eternal Word. I realize the Bible teaches that no one knows the mind of God, and no one is capable of being His instructor, and yet there are times when God chooses to reveal His mind to us puny humans. The Bible, of course, does, in graphic language, tell us of the sordid practice of homosexuality and lesbianism, and the fearful consequences which followed it in Genesis 19, Romans 1, Jude 7, and other places, but nowhere in the Bible is it implied or inferred that any of these men or women actually married the person with whom they committed the act. The Lord Jesus never once gave a single reference to men marrying men or women marrying women, and neither did any Old Testament Prophet, nor any New Testament writer do so. And why not? Could it be that the sacredness of Marriage is such that our Lord and His Apostles deliberately left off mentioning even the probability of such a union as that of two men or two women? Was the probability or the possibility of such a union so far from the thoughts of people from that age that it never crossed their minds, and therefore never made its way into the most sacred of all Books? And if such a union was either probable or possible in that age, did all the writers of the Holy Bible simply forget or neglect to say something about it? I think not. I rather believe that same-sex marriage is absent from the Bible because it is such an abominable thing that God Himself might blush in inspiring good men to describe the sordid and sadistic acts which perverted men and women perform in such a relationship.

But let us employ the common sense with which our Creator endowed us, shall we? The absence of any mention of *"same-sex marriage"* in the Holy Bible tells me that, in reality, there is no such thing as *"same-sex marriage"*. There is no possibility of such a *"marriage"*. Men and women may call it whatever they wish, but it is not a Marriage, in the Scriptural sense, and no minister, called and anointed of God, will have any part in any such ceremony. The union of two persons in holy matrimony is limited to one man and one woman, period. Any union of two persons other than a man and a woman is not a Marriage – it is a Monstrosity, pretending, posing, imitating, and masquerading as a marriage. Two men or two women are incapable of having sex with each other, much less any kind or degree of intimacy. What they do in their bedrooms is not sex – it is sodomy and fellatio, both of which are crimes which were once punishable by imprisonment and/or death. But whenever enough devils get together, and put enough pressure on lawmakers to pass legislation which permits their crimes without any punishment whatsoever, it is an indication that the moral and spiritual condition of that society has eroded to a point wherein divine judgment is imminent, as demonstrated in the fiery destruction of Sodom and Gomorrah.

Chapter Seven

The "g" in Marriage = God.

A good Marriage is a godly marriage, in which God and His Word are the first and final authority, governing every aspect of the relationship from the kiss to the kids to the kitchen, from the basement to the bedroom, from the passion to the porch to the patio, and from the table talk to the pillow talk. Take God out of any one of these areas, and you are left with something which is less than what it could be, and less than what God intended for it to be. The writer has written much about many things which he believes are improper, unseemly, unbecoming, and indecent for human beings to practice, and especially within that most sacred of all human relationships – Marriage. The biggest reason the devil has attacked Marriage so violently, and altered its definition in the minds and hearts of millions is that Marriage was intended to be a living picture of Heaven on Earth, with God and angels smiling upon it with approval and delight.

But sin changed all that. And whenever the devil sees a Marriage which does to some degree reflect the image of Christ and His teaching, he hates that Marriage, and will do everything in his power to corrupt or destroy it.

As with everything in which mankind has a part or interest, Marriage requires that men make decisions, and choices. Some of those decisions and choices are not as easy as others. Men make mistakes. Granted, the consequences of some mistakes are not as grave as the consequences of other mistakes, and I will readily agree that none of us are exempt from, or immune to any of them. All of us are not only susceptible, but prone to err at any given moment. But there is forgiveness with God!

Here I must again send the reader to God's Word: (Ephesians 5:22-33), where the union of a man and a woman is likened unto the union of Christ and His Church. But let me first clarify something I said before. Many have said that Marriage is the most sacred of all *institutions*. Some of my esteemed brethren have reminded me that Marriage is not the most sacred *institution* of all, but that the Church is. And while I do not wish to offend any of my brethren, I yet must be true to my convictions. I do not see either the Church or Marriage as *institutions*, as other men define institutions. And neither do I see the Church or Marriage as organizations, as other men define an organization. I see the Church as a living entity, equated with the living body of Jesus Christ. And Marriage, as God intended for it to be, is supposed to reflect every aspect of the Church in all her glory. These two entities – Marriage and the Church, are to reflect the glory of their Head, Jesus Christ. And there are no other entities, institutions or organizations in the Universe that are capable of reflecting that glory. Is it any wonder, then, that the devil hates these two entities more than any other?

In those verses – Ephesians 5:22-33, the Holy Spirit, using Paul as His instrument, sets forth several *comparisons* between Marriage and the Church, (showing how they are alike,) and unless this student has missed something, there are no *recorded contrasts* (showing how they are different,) between the two. I find that very interesting, to say the least. And could it be that Christ Himself looks upon these two entities, (Marriage and the Church) recognizing little, if any difference between them? Are they so much alike that the Holy Spirit refused *to record* any contrast between them, or did He simply forget to do so? I must leave the reader to answer those questions for himself or herself. There are some contrasts, as will be shown later, but here they are simply not recorded.

The first comparison drawn between Marriage and the Church is that the husband (the head) in a Marriage, is to love his wife *in the same manner* in which Christ (the head) loves His Church. And the proof of his love for his wife should manifest itself in his willingness to lay down his life for her, as Christ laid down His life for the Church. How are we doing so far, gentlemen? But let us never take any earthly comparison with Heavenly things beyond its limitations. Men are capable of loving their wives *in the same manner* that Christ loves His Church, but they can never love her *to the same degree* that Christ loves His Church. A man's love for his wife cannot do for her all that Christ's love did, and is doing for His Church.

And then, Christ, God in flesh, by His death and resurrection, sanctifies and cleanses His bride, and in order to understand this sanctification and cleansing, we must read the rest of verse 26, and all of verse 27. How does Christ sanctify and cleanse His bride? He does so by washing her with the water of His Word – He talks to her, he communicates to her and with her. He has written to her the grandest of all love letters – His Word. And how does the husband sanctify and cleanse his wife, even if she is an unbeliever? He does so by the Word of God. As the Church is set apart by Christ and His Word, she is set apart by Him, unto Him, and for Him, and no other entity can take her place. No other person can do for the Church (His bride) what Christ has done, is doing, and will yet do for her, and no other entity, institution or organization can do for Christ what the Church does. And when a man is joined in holy matrimony to his wife, there is no other man who can do for her what he does, and there is no other woman who can do for him what she does. Are any of us still hanging in there fellows?

In verse 27, we see why Christ died for his bride, and why He continuously sanctifies and cleanses her through His Word – He does so in order that He might present, bring, draw, embrace, and pull her to Himself as a husband draws his wife to himself when he is contemplating intimacy with her. But she must be spotless, her garments must be without wrinkle, which, if otherwise, would suggest or indicate that she had lain with another man. In his eyes she is without blemish, flawless and pure (holy,) in every respect. How about it ladies? Are you ready to take his hand and look him in the eye, knowing that no other man has ever, or will ever touch your body except him? Your two bodies are about to become one, and will this union of your bodies in any way or to any degree defile the other? This man loves his own body, and are you willing to become one with him, knowing your own body has been compromised and violated?

In verse 28, the man loves his wife's body as if it were his own. In loving and **nourishing** the body of his wife, he loves and nourishes his own body. Christ, who is with His bride, one spirit, nourishes Himself and her. He nourishes her with blessings, mercy, grace, love, tenderness, forgiveness, intimacy and countless other graces. She nourishes Him with her love, praise, faithfulness, worship, and countless other spiritual gifts and offerings. In that same verse, the husband **cherishes his wife** in the same manner that Christ cherishes the Church. She is constantly in His thoughts, and all His thoughts of her are precious, holy, and mingled with a godly jealousy, not willing that any other man should touch her. (So much for swingers and wife-swappers). Christ is ever-vigilant to see that his wife has everything that is worthy of the wife of a Prince, and nothing less. Father Abraham sent his servant with ten camels loaded down with gold, silver, all manner of precious things to show Rebecca and her family that his son Isaac was no peasant, but an extremely wealthy man. In a godly marriage, the loving and vigilant husband does everything in his power to make his wife feel like a Queen, and the wife who reverences her husband makes him feel like a King.

The gauntlet which I threw down in an earlier chapter

is still on the ground. Pick it up if you dare, and show me two men or two women who are capable of this kind of love and intimacy, and I will throw my Bible away, and immediately denounce and renounce both the Book and its Author. In verse 30, we, the members of His Church, are members of His body, of His flesh, and of His bones. No two men, and no two women are capable of becoming one flesh, because it is forbidden by the laws of nature, by the laws that govern physiology, and especially by the law of God. The intimacy that exists between a husband and wife was, is, and forever shall be with the intent of producing offspring, and there are no two men or women who are capable of producing offspring through whatever it is they call a "relationship".

The "g" in Marriage stands for God, and without Him in the Marriage, the word is misspelled, and has no meaning whatsoever. Is this what the world wants – a mechanical institution, devoid of warmth, love, intimacy, fun, happiness and longevity? That's what the devil wants, and he has succeeded to a great degree in making millions of copies of his counterfeit currency (marriage licenses). He tried to destroy the first Marriage, and there are some who agree that he did, but not this student. He damaged the first Marriage, but he did not, because he could not, destroy it. That first

Marriage lasted more than nine-hundred years. Marriage is likened unto the Church, and the devil has tried to destroy both, but he has failed on both counts, because neither can be destroyed by either Satan or all of his combined forces. Jesus Christ, the Head of the Church, and the One who founded Marriage, has promised that He will build His church, and the gates of hell shall not prevail against it. And in order for Him to multiply the seed of Abraham as the stars of Heaven for multitude, and as the sand upon the seashore, innumerable, Marriages must and will continue, and there is nothing the devil can do about it.

But that which the devil cannot conquer, he corrupts, or attempts to corrupt. But Christ will not allow His bride to be corrupted, and so He holds the hellhound at bay, deflecting every fiery dart, repelling every unholy insinuation, and by the virtue of His shed blood, denies and denounces every accusation laid against her. He is her Husband, and her great High Priest, ever living to intercede on her behalf, and refuses to behold iniquity in her. He is her Creator and Redeemer, Who bought her unto himself with the utmost price of His own life, and He will not let her go. The bride of Christ is fairer than Eve, and more glorious than angels, and she will walk with Him in white down the avenues of gold into that eternal bedchamber called His

Father's House. The "g" in Marriage stands for God because God is in a true Marriage in the same way He is in the true Church. He is **ever-present** in both, He is **ever-powerful** in both, He is **ever-providing** for both, and He is **ever preserving** both.

And as I have asserted before, when, and only when the man has met the first condition – that of loving his wife even as Christ loves the Church, can he rightfully assume the role of being the head of his wife. Let us for a moment allow that there is such a man. And if there is such a man, God assigns **three responsibilities to the wife** who is married to him, namely (a) *submission* (Ephesians 5:22); (b) *subjection* (Ephesians 5:24); and (c) *reverence* (Ephesians 5:33). Now, before all the ladies blow a fuse, and before all the men get puffed up, let us take a deep breath, and remember that what we are dealing with are *comparisons*, each of which shows how a godly Marriage is *like* that **mystical union** of Christ and His Church. Surely none of you will be angry with the writer is he says the Church is to be in total and constant *submission* to her Head? And is there anyone who will shoot the messenger if he says the Church is to be in constant *subjection* to her Head?

But now we must pause, for we are delving into a great mystery. In the last six words of Ephesians 5:31, Paul wrote - *they two shall be one flesh* (italics mine). And he immediately tells us in verse 32 – this - (two becoming one) is a great mystery. And Paul leaves that mystery alone, right there, offering no instructions, and making no attempt of his own to unravel, explain, or expound upon that mystery. Let us follow the wise example of the beloved Apostle, shall we? And let us, as he did, go on to the point at which he has been aiming since verse one of this fifth chapter.

A single but powerful interjection arrests our attention in the first word of verse 33 – *"Nevertheless"*. Even though the great Apostle admits that he is incapable of explaining the mystery of how two can become one, he yet has more to say which must be said, and he says it. And the wonderful thing about the inspiration of the great Word of God is that those inspired writers were able to say more in a few words than the rest of us can say in an eternity. I beg your prayers and indulgence as I make a feeble attempt to comment on the rest of this single verse – verse 33.

Nevertheless means, even though a married woman is *like the church*, **she is not the** church, and even though a husband is *like Christ*, **he is not Christ,** and even though the union, the marriage itself is *like the union* of Christ and His Church, **it is not that union**. Nevertheless also means that, even though the man is incapable of loving his wife exactly to the same degree and manner in which Christ loves the Church, he is capable of, and responsible for, loving his wife as he loves his own body. And this brings the writer to his final comments on the final statement in this final verse of Ephesians 5. Did the reader notice that I have said nothing yet about the last duty the Apostle imposed upon the wife – namely, ***reverence?***

And before going into that sacred topic, I must say this: In the same way there are no perfect earthly ***illustrations*** of Heavenly things, there are no perfect ***comparisons*** of earthly things to Heavenly things. There are no perfect comparisons between natural things and spiritual things. The very nature of God necessarily prohibits fallen men and fallen creation from exhibiting any perfect comparison to Him whose person and attributes are eternally and infinitely perfect. We can be *like God*, but **we cannot be God**. A married woman can be *like the Church*, **but she cannot be the Church**. Every comparison which the fallen minds of men can concoct or imagine when comparing men and/or things to God, must, at some point, break down, and fall short of divine perfection. No matter how closely men, women and things may resemble God and Heavenly, or spiritual things, there must be at least one contrast, one difference, one disparity in every comparison. There are often several disparities when comparing the natural to the spiritual, but there must be at least one.

Wives are to *reverence* their husbands, but they are to *worship* God, and no one else. The beloved Apostle, inspired of the Holy Spirit, was careful to use the term *"reverence"* and not the term *"worship"*, when imposing this duty upon the wife. May the writer be so bold as to say that in a godly Marriage, with a godly husband rendering due benevolence to his godly wife, she will reverence him – not only because it is *a duty imposed* by the Word of God, but because *it is her delight* to reverence him. Unfortunately, too many men, both Christian and non-Christian, confuse these two terms – reverence and worship, while others make them identical in meaning. But if they are identical, that would eliminate the need for one of them. The Holy Spirit makes no mistakes, and He uses the term *"reverence"* instead of *"worship"* here. Could it be that He did so because He did not want high-minded men to elevate and exalt themselves above their assigned station? I have said before that it is sometimes very difficult for Pastors and counselors to get all the truth from those they counsel, and here is an area in which it is more difficult than in others – getting men to admit that *they want to be worshiped* instead of being reverenced or respected.

There can be reverence without worship, but there cannot be worship without reverence. Reverence must always fall short of worship. Worship must always exceed reverence. Many a mortal monarch, including kings, queens, emperors, princes and princesses throughout the annals of history have demanded that they be worshiped by their subjects. And those who demanded worship from their subjects were never content with mere reverence, considering themselves worthy of more than reverence. Many men and women have lost their heads to the sword, axe, or guillotine for refusing to render worship to the reigning monarch. History records the names of hundreds, perhaps thousands of monarchs who had no reservations whatsoever in demanding and accepting the worship of their subjects. But not until eternity will we know the names of countless others who, having never worn a crown, yet longed to be worshiped. Some of them may be your next door neighbors.

The 'g" in Marriage stands for God, and there has never been another being who is worthy of the worship of his fellow beings, other than God Himself. It may sound unreasonable to the reader of this book for the author to even suggest that some husbands want to be worshiped by their wives and/or children, but again, if only we could see the hidden desires of the human heart, and the longings which lie hidden there! To put it another way, there are men who, while pretending to be content with reverence or respect, would not refuse worship if it were to be offered. And the fact that they would not refuse it means they secretly desire it.

The reverence of which Paul wrote here is nothing more than a high degree of respect - a respect that must be earned by the husband. Not until he meets the conditions imposed upon the husband in these verses is he worthy of this respect, and neither does he have the right to demand it from his wife or children. It is often said of some officers in different branches of the military that they **"commanded"** the respect of the men under their command. This *"commanding"* of the respect of others is **not a demand for it**, but **a deservedness of it**. It is a respect which all of those under his command give him because he has earned it, and they delight to render him that respect. He is the kind of man whose character and care for his men causes them to look up to him, follow his leadership, and speak highly of him, even when not in his presence. This, and nothing either more nor less than this, is the kind of reverence (respect) which God imposes upon the godly wife. And here the writer must often bow his own head in shame, knowing he has not measured up to the high standard set by the Holy Spirit.

Not one of us would hesitate to acknowledge that Christ Jesus is worthy of our praise, worship, reverence, respect, adoration, and admiration, simply because of who He is. He is God in flesh, and like the earthly commander who commands (deserves) the respect of his men, Christ commands (deserves) the reverence and worship of all his followers, and we delight to give Him all our love and allegiance. But how many earthly husbands exhibit the kind of character which causes his wife, his children, his neighbors, and all his acquaintances to render him respect, and speak highly of him even when not in his presence?

Chapter Eight

The "g" in Marriage = Godless.

As surely as there is a marriage, or any other entity which shows any attributes of godliness, the devil will manufacture a counterfeit of it – a counterfeit which so closely resembles the real thing that millions who are either unwary or uninformed are fooled by it. Sad to say, millions are easily taken in with the **_apparent_** beauty and realism of an ungodly institution which sprang from the evil mind of Satan himself. A Godless marriage defines and describes itself – a relationship in which God has no part whatsoever at any time. The writer has already alluded to one such relationship in particular which perfectly defines a *"Godless marriage"*, namely the *"same-sex"* union, which I refuse to acknowledge as a marriage. I am tempted to use the two terms *"Godless"* and *"ungodly"* synonymously here in referring to marriages that exist on paper, but possess not a shadow of the presence of Christ in them. Please correct me if I am wrong, but in my experience with married couples, those marriages which began with no acknowledgement of God whatsoever have, sooner or later, became ungodly in both appearance and conduct. But in an attempt to be as kind as I possibly can, I suppose a Godless marriage could exist without any apparent manifestations of ungodliness, but I seriously doubt it, because in the absence of God in a human relationship, Satan and his lesser devils will not hesitate to insinuate every ungodly act that can be imagined.

A Godless marriage, like the leopard that cannot change its spots, if it never allows God and His Word to become its authority, can never rise above its character. It will forever remain what it is, or become worse than what it is. As with any other relationship involving humans living in close quarters, if there are no godly principles, precepts, or practices by which to operate, that relationship cannot improve on its own, and if there is no positive improvement, I ask, how many other options are there? It is highly unlikely that any human relationship will continue to be exactly what it was in the beginning without any change, either upward or downward. If a marriage does not to any degree become better with the passing of time, there are only two other options – it will either decline, or become stagnant, lifeless, and a miserable routine in which the man and woman simply endure each other. A Godless marriage tends to worsen instead of improving, and as it begins to worsen, the downward spiral is nearly impossible to reverse.

It is within the Godless marriage that we most often find the wife with bruises on her face, arms, neck, and other parts of her body which she is ashamed to show to anyone. It is in the Godless marriage where we most often find children who become gang members, drug addicts, drug pushers, alcoholics, prostitutes, pimps, and thieves. Many a parent has sat across my desk from me with tears in their eyes, showing me ***"before-and-after"*** pictures of their children who were once good-looking young men and women who were, hopefully, destined for a bright and happy future, but who got caught up in the drug culture, and became ***"that other person"***. That other person has rotten teeth, a pock-marked face, disheveled hair, and the countenance of a wild animal. I have sadly gazed at the pictures of young men and women who, at first glance, appeared to be dead with their eyes still open. And many of these youngsters were the children of parents whom I had earnestly tried to persuade to bring to church. Sad to say, many of these parents didn't come to church themselves. But when their children become so far ***"spaced out"*** on drugs, and can no longer cope with reality, some of whom are now suicidal, these same parents want the minister to ***"fix"*** their broken children. They expect the minister to do in fifteen minutes what they failed to do in fifteen or twenty years. Is there any hope at all for the Godless marriage? Yes, there is hope, and His name is Jesus Christ, the One who mends broken hearts and broken homes. And that is the wonder, the inexplicable wonder of His matchless grace – grace that is able to stop a runaway train headed for Hell, turn it around, and put it on the railway Heaven.

Chapter Nine

*The "e" in Marriage = **Endured** vs. **Enduring**.*

    If any author were to attempt to elaborate upon all the teaching of every inspired writer in the Bible on the subject of Marriage, he would probably end up with a book nearly as thick as the Bible itself. In writing this little book, I have deliberately left out some of the teaching of some of the other Apostles and Prophets concerning Marriage with the intent, nay, the hope that each reader will search the Scriptures for himself or herself, and find some of those other golden nuggets of truth. As I have said more than once, if this book does not drive you to the Scriptures, then I have miserably failed as an author who represents our blessed Lord and His Word. As the Scriptures teach, we Christians are to exhort one another, encourage one another, and pray for one another – daily. In more than one instance, the Holy Spirit even uses the term "***provoke***" when instructing us regarding our duties toward our fellow Christians. For example, in Hebrews 10:24 we read:

And let us consider one another to provoke unto love and to good works.

Is that possible – that one individual could consider another in such a way that he or she desires to provoke another individual unto love and good works? What a wonderful world this would be if all of us spent as much time and effort in provoking one another unto love and good works as we spend in provoking one another to anger, hatred, and violence! Without any degree of intent, it may be that this writer, in more than one place in this book, has provoked someone to anger. But regardless of whatever emotion this writer may have provoked in you, if he has not provoked you to study the Scriptures, he has missed his mark. But if that mark has been missed, and the reader is still interested enough to continue reading this book, the writer is yet praying that he may at least provoke you to think more earnestly about this blessed and sacred union called Marriage.

I am glad that God does not allow us to know how many husbands, wives, and children are, at this moment, provoking one another unto wrath, cursing, and countless other forms of evil. How many husbands in America alone are, at this moment, standing in the faces of their wives and/or children, screaming profanity, or threatening violence, with the vile stench of alcohol and/or drugs on their breath? And how many others are cursing their wives for having been two minutes late in putting their supper on the table? And how many children are, at this moment, listening to their parents trade insult for insult (railing for railing), with some resorting to physical violence? And these are only a very few among the countless other scenes that are taking place at this moment in homes around the world. Thank God we cannot see and hear all of it. But God does – every moment of every hour of every day, He sees and hears every insult, every provocation, every harsh word, and ever act of violence. And yet with all of this, many of these marriages continue to exist, day after miserable day, year after miserable year. These are what I call – ***endured marriages.***

And if the dear reader is questioning from what source or sources the author acquired all this information, most of it came from the mouths of married women and men during extensive counseling sessions, and some from the mouths of the children of those parents. There have been more than a few counseling periods in my many years as a Pastor in which I have had to ask an individual to stop talking, because what he or she was saying was too filthy for my ears, let alone for my mind. After listening to some men begin to describe the sadistic behavior in which they have attempted to get their wives to engage in the bedroom, I finally have to raise my hand, stop them, and simply let them know that – "*I get the picture.*" And I am only one Pastor out of many thousands who has had to do this. There is a vast difference between an endured marriage and an enduring marriage. In an endured marriage, the wife and children endure the beatings, the cursing, the neglect, and the physical and mental abuses, many of which are too horrible for decent men and women to utter in public. In the endured marriage, the man and wife endure each other's presence, they endure each other's manners, they endure the loud cursing, the bitterness, and in far too many cases, abominable sexual behavior which resembles that of brute beasts.

Sad to say, but far too many couples who have never known the pure joy of a loving and intimate relationship, have adopted, and conformed to the Hollywood ideal of marriage and sexuality. The bedroom is the place where they vent their frustrations, and pretend to be in love for whatever time it takes to gratify each other's lust. The whole marriage is a sham, a pretense, a façade, pretending to be a loving and enduring relationship. I fully understand that most of what has been written so far on the subject of Marriage has been about the darker aspects of Marriage, and the negative has been emphasized more than the positive, and there is a reason for that, but let me assure the reader that the final chapter of this book will, hopefully, offset, or make up for, all the negative aspects of marriages which the author has mentioned in the preceding chapters. I have painted a pretty dark picture of a relationship which was intended to be the most beautiful and fulfilling of all personal gifts which our great Creator bestowed upon us. I can only hope and pray that a great number of my esteemed colleagues have seen and heard more beautiful stories than the ones I have seen and heard in forty years of ministry. I must be totally honest with the reader, and sadly report that I have seen far more relationships **that do not match** the pure and holy definition and description of Marriage than **the ones that do**. In the privacy of my office, behind a locked door, or in the privacy of my home, or the home of a couple, I have listened to more stories than I care to count – stories that would break the heart of any man who has a heart that can still be touched, and other stories (confessions,) which, to use an old proverb, would make a drunken sailor blush.

    I have listened to couples give me their reasons for staying together in spite of the fact that they have realized their marriage was a huge mistake from the beginning, and has shown no signs of improvement. And in all fairness to the reader, before I close this section, I simply feel I must give you a few of those reasons. And my reason for doing so is the hope that if either your own marriage, or the marriage of someone you know may be on the brink of disaster, perhaps something in these closing chapters will help you, or them, to see exactly where the relationship stands in relation to the Word of God. It may be that you know a marriage or marriages which fit the descriptions I am about to list, describing an endured marriage, versus an enduring marriage.

Many couples endure the relationship for no other reason than the fact that someone told them it's the proper thing to do, regardless of how horrible the conditions might be. I have known other ministers who advised a dear lady to stay with her husband in spite of the fact that he beat her daily, starved her, kept her confined to the house with no outside contact with family or friends, and sexually abused her every day and night. And these same ministers claim that none of these things, nor all of these things together were justification for her leaving him, and their grounds for their advice was that the Scriptures do not allow for divorce under any other condition than the wife committing adultery. Their reasoning is that, regardless of the fact that this marriage should never have happened in the first place, now that it has happened, there is no way out of it, no matter if the abusive husband beats her senseless every day. This is an endured marriage, not an enduring marriage.

And while this Pastor agrees that divorce is a horrible thing, he also believes that staying in an abusive relationship in which there is an endless cycle of physical, mental and moral abuse is far worse than divorce itself. No woman should have to endure that kind of abuse, and I do not believe in a Holy God who would require that she do so because of a piece of paper that should never have been signed by a minister in the first place. And what of the children who are seemingly forever trapped is this living hell? As one dear commentator once said – *"Children would rather be **"from"** a broken home, than be **"in"** a broken home."*

Another type of endured marriage is what us country folks call - *"**a shotgun wedding**."* Here is a marriage which took place under less than perfect circumstances, to say the least. But in all fairness to everyone concerned, I must confess that I have known a few of these "shotgun weddings" to eventually turn out quite well, and become an enduring marriage instead of an endured marriage. These two youngsters may actually have been deeply in love with each other, but made the mistake of putting the cart before the horse. But the fact that a marriage of this type earned the nickname of *"**shotgun wedding**"* makes the marriage speak for itself. There is no sense of discovery on the wedding night, and that purity which could have been preserved for the honeymoon is now gone forever. But again, in fairness to everyone, let it be established that many of these marriages would not have happened had it not been for the father of the bride holding a shotgun on the groom. Another variation of the "shotgun wedding" is one in which the couple has confessed that they engaged in sexual activity before being married, then discovered the girl was pregnant, and got married without either parent knowing she was pregnant until a few months after the ceremony. The two got married because they felt "***they had to get married***', instead of "***wanting to get married.***" And while this marriage may, or may not, – "***work out***" eventually, it can never be what it could have been with just a little abstinence on the part of both parties.

Another type of endured marriage which other couples have confessed to enduring is the one which is endured – "***because of the kids.***" By their own confession, these folks have said that the only thing which prevents the marriage from being dissolved (legally) is that there is a child or children involved, and they don't want the children to have to go through the trauma of seeing their parents divorced. And while this may seem highly commendable, and a noble sentiment on the surface, may this author immediately object, and say that this marriage has already been dissolved, in the moral sense. This kind of marriage, of course, seems far better than the one in which the husband is a monster, and beats his wife and children, and there would probably be very few ministers who would recommend that the marriage be legally dissolved – *"for the children's sake."* I have heard some ministers say that, even though the man and woman may not have been helplessly in love with each other at the beginning, now that a child is involved, they should stay together, and perhaps *"learn to love each other"* somewhere down the road. I am not saying this is impossible, but I will adamantly contend that it is highly improbable. Some ministers and counselors, when dealing with a situation like this, remind the man and wife that they now have a responsibility (the child or children) which they must both accept, and do the best they can to *"make the marriage work"*. And while there are some who would characterize this relationship as an enduring marriage, I must, with all due respect, call it an endured marriage.

And now the writer must pause once more, for there is a great deal of reckoning to be done here. Yes, we must consider the children and their future. And yes, we must allow that two persons, living under the same roof for any number of years, and realizing they have made a mistake, but are willing to compensate for that mistake at the cost of their own happiness, may, over a period of time, actually come to love each other deeply. It has happened, and can happen again. And when it happens, I will be the first man to congratulate that couple for the sacrifices they have made for the sake of the children. And I will cautiously agree that a marriage of this type, can, **with help from above,** evolve into an enduring marriage. But I must also caution the reader of the fact that the likelihood of a marriage of this kind working out for the good of all concerned is very small. But we live in a society whose motto is – *"all's well that ends well."* This, of course, means that as long as there is a *"happy ending"* to the story, the happiness at the end makes all the unhappiness of many years' worth the enduring of that unhappiness. I'll let the reader make his or her own choice of how much, if any, of that statement he or she wishes to accept. But wouldn't it have been far better if the couple had simply taken the time to learn more about each other, and made certain that what they felt for each other was love, and not heightened emotions, puppy love, or infatuation? And would it not have been far better if they had abstained from premarital sex, and waited until the wedding night?

I pray each reader can put a big bold **YES** at the end of those last two questions.

I am desperately wanting to bring this section of the book to a close, and move on to what I pray will be the most positive, and cheerful chapter in the book, entitled The Enduring Marriage. But I cannot in good conscience leave out these last few paragraphs describing one more "endured marriage". And again, I am simply passing on to the reader things which I have seen and heard from the opposite side of my desk, coming from the broken hearts of both men and women who have literally "endured" one of the types of marriage I have cited above. And let me assure the reader – I have heard it for more than forty years now, almost on a weekly basis. And I guess I should also add that not all the couples I have met in counseling sessions were young couples – their ages ranged from the teens to the seventies. And in case any reader is wondering – Yes, I have had individuals (men only) in their eighties come to me with stories from their bedrooms – stories that made me blush.

This last type of *"endured"* marriage is one which has puzzled this Pastor for as long as I have been in the ministry. It is a marriage which continues to exist in spite of everything either the couple themselves do *to each other*, or imagine *against each other*, and in spite of everything the devil suggests they do **with each other**. In this relationship, nothing is off limits in any room of the house, not even the language each person uses, and nothing is reserved until the children are absent. This is what our society, to a large degree, has accepted as an "open marriage", in which every word and every action is open to the couple's own definition and interpretation. It is also an open marriage in the sense that the door is always open for either the husband or wife to go and have an affair with another man or woman, then come back through the same open door, and resume the ungodly practices in which they indulge on a daily basis. In many of these relationships, near the beginning of them, on the surface, there seems to be nothing amiss, and a visit to that home might leave the visitor with the impression that this is a perfectly normal American household, and the couple is "*living the dream*", and destined to live – "*happily ever after.*"

But upon leaving that home, no sooner does the visitor get in his car, and all hell breaks loose inside that house! There is screaming, yelling, cursing, and a "*knock-down-drag-out*" brawl, with a protracted session of "*make-up*" sex to follow, which, in many cases, becomes as physically violent as the brawl itself. Many couples have admitted that every window in their house had to be replaced at one time or another, and some several times, as a result of objects being thrown at each other's heads during a heated fight. I am not exaggerating to any degree in saying that many couples have had to replace nearly every piece of furniture in their house as a result of physical violence between the man and wife. And in many of these family brawls, children were present, seeing and hearing everything. I don't even want to remember how many times a young person has come to me secretly, weeping, while telling me the sordid details of a recent episode of physical violence in their home. And even sadder, many of these young men and women, most of them teenagers, have heard so much filthy language from the mouths of their parents, they themselves have adapted to it, and know of no other means of expressing themselves than to repeat what they have heard.

    I have had to raise my hand and stop countless numbers of young men and women from proceeding with their graphic accounts of what they have seen and heard in their homes, simply because my own ears found it too repulsive to endure. And while this writer is on be subject, he may as well finish what he started, hoping and praying that what he has to say will somehow, someday, have a positive effect upon someone. I have alluded to a few different kinds of marriage, each of which has the propensity and the probability of ending in disaster. But some of these marriages go far beyond being a disaster – some of them end in death. One such relationship, in which both the man and woman died needlessly, happened to hit very close to home – a sister and her *"live-in"* boyfriend killing each other. One used a knife, the other a rifle, but both died a violent and horrible death, and I have no idea whether either of them was saved before they died. We only need to watch the six o'clock news, or pick up a newspaper and read the staggering statistics which show how many thousands more of these deadly relationships are ending this way every day, somewhere in our own country, and around the world.

Yes, I have said enough about the darker, negative side of Marriage, and it is time to move on to better and happier things. With what the reader has read so far, I have no doubt that he or she, or someone you know, could add yet more chilling details to what this author has written. And if the reader is anything like myself, you would probably rather not add anything more, but perhaps turn the page, and try to send all of this to a secret file in the back of your mind, where you can open it again someday, and remind yourself, or someone you love, of the harsh realities that afflict the human race on a daily basis. But for now, let's file it all away somewhere in the deep recesses of our brains, and behold a much brighter picture of that blessed and sacred "institution" we call Marriage. Let's look at The Enduring Marriage.

It would not be fair to anyone, and it would dishonor our great God for me to go much farther without inserting what I believe may be one of the most important paragraphs in this book. There have been some marriages which began as a bad idea, which were built upon less than perfect materials, which had no definitive plan, and were, from all appearances, doomed to failure from the beginning, but, later found redemption in God and His Word, and became beautiful pictures of a loving and enduring Marriage. This, of course, clearly demonstrates the power of grace, which is able to change lives, and mend broken hearts and broken homes. It has been my joy to see the love and grace of God in action, turning troubled marriages into trusting marriages. And in the same way Christ saves and changes the heart of the individual, He saves many a couple, and their children from the devastation of a broken home.

When Christ and His Word become the guiding principles of a marriage that was once headed for destruction, that same marriage is transformed into something lovely to behold. It is not counseling or sound advice that saves the soul – it is Christ who saves the soul, and it is not counseling or sound advice that saves a ruined marriage – it is Christ Himself who does so.

Chapter Ten

The "e" in Marriage = Enduring.

If the reader hasn't already figured out what is the stance of the writer on the subject of Marriage, there would probably be very little else the writer could add that would finally establish that stance. But for the record, I am a conservative, old-school, dyed-in-the-wool Baptist preacher with more than forty years of ministry under my belt. As for my beliefs, positions, and convictions, whether religious, moral, or political, very little has changed since the day the Lord Jesus saved my soul – Sunday evening, August 24th, 1974, at the Dripping Springs Missionary Baptist Church, situated on Callebs Creek, in the foothills of Southeastern Kentucky. As I have already likened a Marriage unto the relationship between Christ and His Church, let me now liken a Marriage unto the relationship that exists between Christ and the individual believer. One of the most long-standing controversial topics that exists among Christian brethren is the age-old argument for, or against the eternal security of every believer in Christ Jesus. There are those who believe and teach that the salvation of the soul is a conditional salvation, which, under certain circumstances, may be forfeited. This teaching says, in essence, that the believer, once saved, must endure to the end, to the very last breath of his or her life, without committing another sin in order to retain that salvation. But if the believer should commit any sin between the moment of salvation and death, he or she may, or may not, be saved again.

At the opposite end of that spectrum is the belief that once the soul is saved, it can never be lost again under any circumstance, but is eternally secure in Christ, kept by His own power, preserved for eternity. In the former case, simply stated, the believer – "**must endure** unto the end *in order to be saved* in the end." In the latter case, the believer – "**will endure** unto the end, *because he is saved.*" And having been in the ministry for more than forty years, I can assure the reader that this disagreement will not be settled for as long as there are humans on the Earth. And if the dear reader wishes for this poor student to attempt to settle it here and now, that is about as likely as me becoming the first man to land on Saturn. But be that as it may, I do have a position, nay, a conviction on the matter, a conviction which I will now attempt to incorporate into this last chapter – The

Enduring Marriage.

In his most famous of all speeches, the Gettysburg Address, President Abraham Lincoln said – *"Fourscore and seven years ago our forefathers brought forth upon this continent a new nation, conceived in liberty, and dedicated to the proposition that all men are created equal. Now we are engaged in a great civil war, testing whether that nation, or any nation, so conceived and so dedicated, can long endure."* Our nation has endured, and Oh how much she has endured! But will she, can she endure much longer? Her name endures, but not much else upon which she was founded has endured. Her founding principles are being bent, twisted, stretched and manipulated in an attempt to satisfy the insatiable appetites of the greedy, and to accommodate the modernistic idealism of those who do not believe in God and His Word.

In the case of the believer, when he is saved, he will endure temptation, he will endure persecution, he will endure hardships, he will endure sickness and pain, he may endure the loss of friends and finances, but none of these things individually, nor all of these things together can change that enduring relationship that exists between his soul and Christ. His relationship to Christ endures – not because he has endured all these things, but in spite of the fact that he has endured all these things. It is not his enduring of all these things that holds his soul secure, it is Christ Himself who holds his soul secure. And so it is with an enduring Marriage – it will endure hardships, it will endure suffering, it will endure periods of highs and lows, it will endure anything and everything which the world, the flesh, and the devil can throw at it, but the Marriage itself will endure, not as a result of having endured all those things, but as a result of that which brought the man and woman together in the first place – the presence of God in the Marriage. The soul that has Christ in it endures because of Him, and the Marriage that has Christ in it endures for the same reason – because He is there.

In an *endured marriage,* the individuals **endure one another**, in an *enduring Marriage*, they **enjoy one another.** And this same difference exists between religion and salvation. In religion, the person who practices it **endures** all its laws and precepts, its rules and regulations, its do's and don'ts, feeling that he must endure them in order to remain saved. In salvation, the believer **enjoys his salvation and his Savior, not because he must, but because he wants to.** In an endured marriage, the individuals **test each other**; in and enduring Marriage, they **tantalize each other**. In an endured marriage the individual's **rail on each other**; in an enduring Marriage **they ravish each other.** In an endured marriage **there is fear;** in an enduring Marriage **there is faith**. The endured marriage spawns **sorrow;** the enduring Marriage spawns **serenity**. The endured marriage thrives upon **horror;** the enduring Marriage thrives upon **honor.** In an endured marriage, **the children suffer;** in an enduring marriage, **the children sing**.

In an enduring Marriage, the couple enjoys the fruits of **enduring principles**, principles which have stood the test of time, and have withstood the storms of time. The guiding principles that hold an enduring Marriage together do so because they are based upon the infallible Word of God. And surely we can all agree that the strongest principle in any human relationship is love. The enduring Marriage is based upon the principle of **unconditional love**; the endured marriage is based upon the principle of **uncontrolled lust**. The enduring Marriage incorporates the enduring principle of **faithfulness**; the endured marriage incorporates the principle of **falsehood**. The principles that hold an enduring Marriage together are **infused;** the principles that hold an endured marriage together are **enforced.** In the endured marriage, the couple sees trouble coming, they *compare the trouble to themselves,* and say, *"we are no match"*; in the enduring Marriage, the couple sees trouble coming, *they compare the trouble to Christ,* and say – *"He's more than a match."* In an enduring Marriage, the couple **safely trusts each other**, in the endured marriage, **they seldom trust anyone**. In an enduring Marriage, **love unites the individuals,** in an endured marriage, **love escapes them**. In the enduring Marriage, **the bed is never defiled,** in the endured marriage, **the bed is never decent.**

Enduring principles guide and support the enduring Marriage because those principles themselves are based upon an ***enduring premise*** – the premise that God keeps His Word. Since the Word of God is infallible and inerrant, whatever is written therein must necessarily be true, and whatever is promised therein must necessarily come to pass, without fail. The husband who has a virtuous wife never needs to doubt her love for him, nor her faithfulness to him, and if he believes the Word of God, he must believe the promise that – she will do him good and not evil all the days of her life (Proverbs 31:12). ***The promise*** that she will do him good and not evil all the days of her life is based upon ***the premise*** that God keeps His Word. Simply put, the ***enduring Marriage*** rests upon ***enduring principles,*** based upon an ***enduring premise,*** out of which flow ***enduring promises.***

If you the reader were writing this book, what would you say the very first enduring principle would be that holds an enduring marriage together? I doubt that anyone in his or her right mind would place any other principle ahead of Love. No matter what else a human relationship may possess, if it does not possess mutual love, there is no hope for that relationship. There is no substitute for love, and regardless of what men and women try to substitute in the place of love, and no matter how much that substitute may resemble love, it can never rise above what it is – it can never become love as love is defined in the Holy Bible. Whenever young engaged couples come to me for premarital counseling, once I get past that stage of trying to talk them out of it, if they are still insistent upon being married, I always ask the same first question – "Do you love each other?" I fully understand why many other ministers might not ask that question, but I do, because I want to see the look in their eyes in that split second after the question is asked. Believe me when I say that I have seen reactions to that question which would make the devil blush with shame. I've had men and women curse me for asking that simple question – "Do you love each other?" I've seen others get up and walk out of my office, muttering profanity under their breath, while calling me some unsavory names. But there have been others who smiled, looked at each other, held each other's hand, and lovingly affirmed to me and to each other that they did indeed love each other, without saying a word.

I get a pretty good sense of how the relationship is going simply from the amount of time the couple is willing to spend listening to their Pastor ask, and answer questions. Those who are in a heated rush to hear the Pastor say he will perform the ceremony without asking too many questions are the ones who, more often than not, wind up going to either another minister, a judge, or someone who has obtained a ministerial license online, without any formal training or experience in the realm of Marriage. These are also the ones who, more often than not, end up enduring each other for a lifetime instead of enjoying each other for a lifetime, or, they simply get a divorce, and move on to what they hope will be greener pastures.

Once in a while, a few couples, when asked that question – (do you love each other?) respond with something like – *"Of course we love each other. We wouldn't be here if we didn't love each other; why do you ask?"* And then I tell them why I asked, by giving them three examples of an enduring Marriage. Some are willing to sit and listen patiently, while others soon make it clear that they'd really rather not hear any more examples of an enduring Marriage, and they leave. My first example of an enduring Marriage is the one that was responsible for me being born – the enduring Marriage of my father and mother – Robert and Ethel Keene-Jones, whose Marriage survived World War One, The Great Depression, World War Two, Korea, Vietnam, and fourteen children. They buried five of their fourteen children. When my Dad became bedfast, and couldn't feed himself, my Mom fed him. When he couldn't bathe himself, she bathed him. When he couldn't clean himself, she cleaned him. She sat by his bedside, wiping the sweat from his brow, kissing his cheek, showing him how much she loved him. She was there when he took his last breath. She sat by his casket in their living room, receiving friends and neighbors who came to pay their respects. My Mom and Dad were married when Mom was fourteen, and Dad was seventeen. Mom accepted the Lord Jesus Christ when she was fifteen. Dad was saved when he was sixty years old. My Mom believed the premise that God keeps His Word, she lived by the principles set forth in His Word, and she claimed the promises in His Word. Not one child in fourteen ever saw a hungry day, and not one ever went without food, clothing, or shelter.

If the young engaged couple is still there, and listening, I move on to another enduring Marriage - my own, which has now lasted almost forty-nine years. Just about everything that can be hurled at a married couple has been hurled at my wife and I. My wife, Carolyn Jordan-Jones, is one of the most godly women I have ever known, and virtuous in every respect. The first five years of our marriage was tumultuous, to say the least. She endured my drinking, my cursing, and my ungodliness, while maintaining her dignity, grace, and uncompromising principles by which she was raised. Our marriage was on the brink of destruction until the Lord Jesus saved both of us, and our Marriage. We now have three children, six grandchildren, and one great granddaughter. And there is no power in heaven or hell, or anywhere in between that can come between us, although many have tried.

    And finally, if the couple is still listening, I tell them the Biblical story of the Prophet Hosea and his wife Gomer, a marriage which, more vividly than any other, is a picture of the relationship between Christ and His Church. The reader will do well to read, nay, to study that Book before proposing or accepting a proposal of marriage. The Prophet is commanded by God to love a woman who has committed fornication, whoredom, and adultery. Her life has been reduced to that of a slave being auctioned off to the highest bidder, and yet her Husband buys her back, takes her unto himself, gives himself to her, and loves her as if she had never sinned at all.

So I bought her to me for fifteen pieces of silver, and for an homer of barley, and an half homer of barley: And I said unto her, Thou shalt abide for me many days; thou shalt not play the harlot, and thou shalt not be for another man, so will I also be for thee (Hosea 3:2,3).

And who would dare to write a book on Marriage without sending the reader to the incomparable love story penned by the inspired King Solomon – Song of Solomon? Here the enduring Marriage is defined and described in terms which no un-inspired tongue can speak, and no un-inspired hand can write. In chapter one the bride expresses her love for Christ, and confesses her own deformity. She prays to be directed to His flock, and He answers her prayer, directing her to the shepherd's tents. He expresses his love to her in extending great and precious promises to her, and in mutual adoration, they congratulate one another. In chapter two, the Bride and Groom express their mutual love, as the Bride expresses her profession, faith, hope and calling. In chapter three we see the battle the church must fight in the bodily absence of her Love, Whom she seeks diligently till she finds Him, and glories in His power, His provision, and His presence. In Chapter four, Christ, the Groom, declares the many graces of His Bride, and shows His love to her, while she prays to be made fit for His presence. In chapter five, Christ stands at the door of the undefiled bedchamber of His undefiled Bride, knocking, and calling to her, awakening her. She rises to bid Him enter, but He is gone into the streets of the city, where He is ill-treated by the townsmen. And though the Bride does not see Him bodily, she yet describes His glorious body in graphic detail. In chapter six the Church again professes her faith in Christ, as He describes the inimitable beauties and graces of His Bride. And as if there are not enough words by which to express His love for her, and never enough to describe her grace and beauty, He adds yet another chapter, full of vividly descriptive terms that describe each glorious part of her glorious body, as she, in turn, assures Him of her love for Him. And in the final chapter – chapter eight, the Church lovingly declares her love for Christ in terms which no Hollywood actor, actress, producer or director can fully capture on film.

In verses six and seven of this last chapter, we see the kind of love which creates, builds, and sustains an enduring marriage. It is a love that is strong as death. But what does the Holy Spirit want us to gather from that statement – *love is strong as death*? The same writer who wrote this beloved

Song tells us – no man has power in the day of death (Ecclesiastes 8:8b). The will to live is stronger in some men than in others, but in the day of death, not even the strongest will can hold the grim reaper at bay. Death is stronger than the strongest man, and love is strong as death, therefore love is stronger than the strongest man. ***To the extreme which death goes*** in order to overcome the will to live, ***to that extreme love goes*** in order to overcome the powers that would tear asunder an enduring marriage. Within the divine love of God for His people is a divine jealousy, a jealousy which breaks His heart when His people go a whoring after other gods; a jealousy which, if not perceived by anointed eyes, would resemble cruelty on the human level. So jealous is God over His people that He will resort to divine wrath upon any and all who would afflict, offend, or seduce His beloved Bride.

In verse seven of chapter eight (Song of Solomon), we read:

Many waters cannot quench love, neither can the floods drown it: if a man would give all the substance of his house for love, it would utterly be contemned.

Here are three metaphors, three examples of the power and endurance of love. (1) It is like a fire which ***cannot be quenched by many waters.*** Can our finite minds imagine a fire so vehement it defies every means by which men attempt to put it out? But I know of no better way to illustrate the love of God than by copying the last verse of that beloved old hymn – The Love of God. That last verse was discovered on the wall of an asylum, left there by a man who was diagnosed with dementia –

Could we with ink the oceans fill, and were the skies of parchment made;

Were every stalk on earth a quill, and every man a scribe by trade;

To write the love of God above would drain the oceans dry,

Nor could the scroll contain the whole, though stretched from sky to sky.

(2) Floods cannot drown love. Will the reader notice that those things which are mentioned as being incapable of quenching love (many waters) or drowning love (floods) are plural. Many are the *"waters"* that would put out the fire of love if they could, and many are the *"floods"* that would drown it. We know, of course, the writer is using figurative language here – he is not thinking of literal waters or literal floods, but of all those things which would extinguish the flame of love if they could, and all those things which would suffocate the love of a man and wife if they could, but none of them can. No individual thing or person, nor any number of things and persons can extinguish or suffocate the love that binds a husband and wife in an enduring marriage. The waters of affliction and adversity cannot quench the flame of love that burns in the hearts of true lovers, and neither can the floods of temptation, testing, and trials drown it.

(3) The love that makes an enduring marriage *cannot be bought at any price.* A love that can be bought is contemptible, worthless, despicable, disdainful, scornful, and unworthy of a single moment of honest consideration.

Another enduring principle which cannot be absent from an enduring marriage is *faithfulness.* Here is another sacred term which has suffered much at the hands of modernistic ideology. Some of the saddest comments this Pastor has ever heard came from some fellow employees while we ate lunch together many years ago. One young man, in a single statement, told me all I needed to know about the strength (I should say weakness) of his marriage. His own words were – *"I'll be faithful to her (his wife) till I find someone better looking."* Another young man commented – *"I'll be faithful as long as she does what I tell her to do."* And not to be outdone, another young man chimed in – *"I'll be faithful to my wife as long as she gives me what I want, when I want it."* Among the many contemptible things in all three of these statements is a common denominator in all three, namely, a condition which must be met by the wife in order to receive the ongoing love of her husband. Here were three marriages, all of which were simply going through the motions, keeping up appearances, and in which the husband was simply waiting for a convenient moment to dump his wife, and find another as soon as possible. That is not faithfulness.

One of the most valuable tools I learned to use in Bible College was that of defining terms negatively before defining them positively. In other words, *learn what the term does not mean*, and then *what it does mean will stand out more clearly.* For example, some men, and I might be safe in saying most men, define faithfulness in marriage as simply being there with the wife on a daily basis, working and supporting the family, and not cheating on her with any other woman. And while that sounds like a fair enough definition of faithfulness, it does not define it with complete accuracy. Faithfulness is not just being there performing certain duties, and neither is it simply refusing to have an affair with another woman. A man can be unfaithful to his wife sitting in front of a television, a computer, a cell phone, or while reading a book or magazine. More than a few husbands have confessed that they have been unfaithful to their wives even in their own bedrooms. It has been my unhappy lot to hear wives say their husbands called out the name of another woman while being intimate with her. Others have left their husbands in the middle of the night after hearing him call another woman's name in his sleep. Many husbands are quite content or even proud of themselves if they have been faithful – *in a few things*. Some go so far as to grant themselves a license to be unfaithful in a few things, because they have been *somewhat faithful* in others. Positively - **Faithfulness in marriage means being faithful in all things, at all times, under all circumstances.** So, how are we doing in the "*faithfulness*" department, brethren?

My old heart pains me a bit at times when I must say and do things which run contrary to "*traditional*" thinking and acting. It is never my wish or intention to deliberately offend another Christian brother or sister, and neither do I cherish getting engaged in political, religious, or moral controversies simply for the sake of "*proving my point*". One great lesson I learned from a dear Professor and friend was – "*I'd much rather win a soul than win an argument*". We would do well if we spent more time **declaring our convictions** than we spend in **defending our positions.** Declaring our convictions is called preaching, defending our positions is called quarreling. Sadly, many ministers fail to realize that some folks in their congregations actually know the difference between preaching convictions and defending positions. But what does this have to do with Marriage, you may ask?

Let me put it this way – if we, as ministers of Christ and His Gospel ask, insinuate, or demand that the man and woman promise, vow, to be faithful to one another, should we not hold ourselves to the same standard? Before we agree to perform any ceremony, we need to ask ourselves some serious questions. Have we been faithful in asking some personal questions about each individual's personal relationship to Christ? Have we been faithful to God and His Word by declaring the whole counsel of God to this couple and their respective families? Have we been faithful to the couple in clearly stating our Scripturally-based stance on every aspect of the marriage relationship? Have we been faithful in asking the hard questions concerning premarital sex? Have we been faithful in clearly stating our position on divorce? And if we have asked ourselves these questions, and find that we have not been faithful in our ministerial duties to God and man, then we need to ask ourselves one more question - How faithful can a marriage be which was solemnized by an unfaithful minister?

If we do not have any convictions on the subject of Marriage, we have no business performing ceremonies; we have no business preaching or teaching on the subject; and we definitely have no business writing on the subject. One dear Pastor once reminded me that all of us in the ministry have three things – beliefs, positions, and convictions. He quickly added that – *"beliefs change, and positions shift, but convictions are those things for which we are willing to die rather than deny them."* And with that Pastor's statement, we, all of us, must either agree or disagree, for there is no middle ground. There are plenty of beliefs and positions, but how many of us have deep, uncompromising convictions for which we refuse to apologize, or for which we are willing to die? If this Pastor has not established his beliefs, positions, and convictions on the subject of Marriage by now, it is doubtful that he ever will. But just in case I may have failed to convey to the reader what my heart knows to be true, I beg your indulgence for a few pages more, as I attempt to finalize this small work. How strongly do we believe what we profess to believe? Let me illustrate with a hypothetical situation. A Pastor loudly and forcefully proclaims from his pulpit that he is vehemently against same-sex marriage. The powers that be pass a law which states that he must perform a wedding ceremony for a same-sex couple, or face fines and/or imprisonment, and his church will lose its tax-exempt status, or be closed, or both. How does the Pastor respond to this law? I know what my response would be, and it would be without a moment's hesitation.

It is highly unlikely that in my lifetime we will come to that point wherein a minister's life is threatened if he chooses not to perform same-sex marriages, but let us not become so complacent or naïve as to think it can't happen. And if it were to come to that, how faithful would all we ministers be to our professed beliefs, positions, and convictions? Would we, like John the Baptist, at the risk of having our heads lobbed off, stand in the face of a king and tell him it was unlawful for him to take his brother's wife? John had more than beliefs and positions; he had deep convictions about **the sanctity of marriage**. John, with only the Scriptures of the Old Testament to stand upon, stood firmly upon what he knew to be true and right. It was for his stance on the sanctity of marriage, and for nothing else that John was beheaded. How, then, can we who now have both the Old and New Testaments, take Marriage so lightly as to join two men or two women in wedlock without a blush of shame? If faithfulness is an enduring principle in an enduring marriage, it demands faithfulness on the part of every person involved, including the minister who solemnizes the ceremony. I simply cannot overemphasize the importance of the role the minister plays in performing wedding ceremonies. Whether he realizes it or not, when he agrees to perform a wedding ceremony, the minister takes on a grave responsibility. He is about to engage in a work for which he must someday give an account to God for having done it. And as I begin to think about how to end this small work, I must first acknowledge, it could have been done far better by almost anyone else who knows Christ as Lord, and who is well-acquainted with His eternal Word.

I have two more enduring principles which I believe must be part of an enduring marriage, two principles without which the marriage cannot survive. So far I have mentioned only two principles – love and faithfulness. I have placed great emphasis upon the necessity of both of these principles in an enduring marriage. The reader may also have noticed that I have placed strong emphasis upon the responsibilities of all the parties involved, including the minister. Having been a minister myself for forty years, I have learned much through both experience and study, and yet I have so much more to learn, and not much time in which to learn it. Whatever I have written in these few pages, I have written with the fear of God in my heart, and the glory of God as my ultimate goal. If I have not honored and glorified my Lord in this book, then it is utterly worthless, and has been a total waste of time and effort. But if I have exalted Him, even by accident, and if I have accidentally or intentionally written something that someday proves to be a small blessing to my fellow man, then this work will not have been in vain. Only time will tell. If the dear reader has come this far with me, let me take this opportunity to thank you and congratulate you for your patience. If you are still reading this book, I am deeply honored and humbled for your longsuffering.

These last two principles I am about to incorporate into this book are **"*honor*"** and **"*patience*"**. The reader may recall something I wrote about finding fault with the wording of most "standardized" or "traditional" wedding ceremonies. And while the term "honor" is still used in some ceremonies, it too has been deleted from many ceremonies I have witnessed. And while I have already agreed that I do not wish to re-write the "traditional" ceremony, I yet feel that we do the couple an injustice if we fail to include these two terms – honor, and patience. Some folks, of course, may object by saying that both honor and patience ought to be foregone conclusions – things which the couple simply take for granted in a marriage. Unfortunately, there are too many things which are taken for granted in a marriage. Those whose marriages began as a bad idea, and evolved into a lifelong epic of misery and unhappiness, if they would confess, would most likely tell us that neither the minister nor anyone else said anything about honoring one another, or being patient with one another, either before, during, or after the ceremony.

During my waning years as a minister, I have performed fewer and fewer wedding ceremonies with each passing year. There is more than one reason for the decline. I suspect this book may spell the end for me in performing another ceremony. There are those who say I am too old-fashioned, too stringent, and too narrow-minded to be called upon to solemnize their marriage. But there are others, a few others, who will call no one else. But if I am to attain my self-imposed goal of 101 pages for this book, I must concentrate upon these last two principles – honor and patience, and say as much as I can in the few pages I have left. Imagine with me, if you can, a ceremony:

"Mr. Jones, do you promise in the sight of God and these witnesses to love, honor, and cherish this woman, to be faithful to her, and be patient with her, in sickness and in health, for richer or for poorer, for better or for worse, for as long as you both shall live?"

Let the man think on it for a few moments, and if or when you get and "I do", from him, you repeat the same vows to the woman:

"And Miss Jordan, do you promise in the sight of God and these witnesses to love, honor, and cherish this man, to be faithful to him, and be patient with him, in sickness and in health, for richer or for poorer, for better or for worse, for as long as you both shall live?"

I ask – what would be wrong, offensive, or inadmissible in that short but sweet ceremony? After all, if the man and woman are willing to vow their love and faithfulness to each other, there should be no difficulty with, or objection to, vowing to honor and be patient with each other. If I can love you for a lifetime, and be faithful to you for a lifetime, I should have no problem in honoring you and being patient with you for that same lifetime. But as the reader has already gathered from what you have read so far, this poor writer likes to define his terms before incorporating them into the work itself. Let's deal with **"*honor*"** first. In a marriage, an enduring marriage, what does it mean for a husband to honor the wife, and for the wife to honor the husband?

Of the many definitions of honor which I find in the dictionary, here are a few which I feel best define the honor that is expected from the man and wife toward each other:

Honor: 1. glory, fame, renown. 2. Credit for acting well, good name. 3. A nice sense of what is right and proper. 4. Sticking to action that is right, or that is usual or expected. 5. Great respect, high regard. 6. Rank, dignity, distinction. 7. Chastity, virtue.

The man honors his wife when he (a) ***honors her person.*** She is not a mechanical tool for him to use for his own personal benefit and pleasure, then hang her up on a nail or hook until he needs her again. You are one flesh, and the manner in which you honor your wife is the manner in which you honor yourself. And in the manner, and to the degree that you either honor or dishonor your wife, you honor or dishonor yourself. Furthermore, if or when you honor or dishonor your wife, you not only honor or dishonor yourself, you also honor or dishonor God, His Word, your vows, and Marriage itself. She is not your personal slave, who must come at your beck and call, and do your bidding. She is your partner who shares in every aspect of your own life. You honor her person when you speak highly of her both in public and in private, and those who hear her name fall from your lips know that she is special to you in every respect.

The man honors his wife when he (b) ***honors her purity.*** This student of the Scriptures cannot find enough adjectives with which to define or describe the high honor of mutual purity between a man and woman who are about to be wed. A man honors his wife's purity by keeping himself pure for her until the wedding day. He also honors her purity by never suggesting that she compromise her own purity for his gratification before the wedding day. Paradise lost may eventually be regained, but **purity lost can never be regained**. And yet it seems to be the most difficult task of all for Pastors and parents to instill in young people the virtue of maintaining sexual purity until marriage. In today's society, sexual purity is something which has become almost archaic - few people seem to know what it means, because so few people are ever taught what it means. Like so many other sacred things, purity seems to have been lost in obscurity. But the saddest thing of all is that most of the young persons who have either come to me on their own, or who have been sent to me by their parents, don't seem to care about sexual purity before marriage. They don't care about their own sexual purity, and neither does it bother them at all if the person they are dating, or planning on marrying has engaged in sexual activities with any number of partners. But this old-fashioned preacher still maintains that where there is no purity, there is no honor; if one is lost, the other is lost.

A man honors his wife when he (c) ***honors her privacy.*** There is nothing more dishonorable to a wife than having her husband broadcast to other men what goes on in their bedroom. And there is nothing more sickening or reprehensible to the ears of a decent man than hearing another man brag of his adventures behind closed doors. Some men do not realize that when they are speaking of their wives, they are speaking of themselves also, for the two are now one. Give me your estimate of your wife, and I will give you your estimate of yourself. And if the reader is wondering whether there are such men who would sink to that level of indecency, wonder no more; for there are such men, and there are such women, and they are not confined to any particular culture, race, or nationality. These are the sort of men and women who have come into my office from time to time, thinking that I, as a minister, should be willing to sit and listen to the sordid, sickening details of what happened in their bedrooms last week. I am proud to say that I have disappointed them in refusing to listen to such indecency.

A man honors his wife when he (d) ***honors her position***. Although God Himself declares the two to be one, yet each one occupies a specific and distinct position in the marriage relationship, and each one is admonished to fulfill specific duties within that position. And here is just one more divine prohibition against same-sex marriages. While watching a certain show on television recently, a certain young lady was asked if she was married. My stomach turned when she responded – "*Yes, I am married to my lovely wife*...(and she called the name of her "wife"). My wife and I looked at each other stunned, but said nothing, shaking our heads in disbelief and disgust. It is not possible for a woman to have a wife, and it is equally impossible for a man to have a husband. The position which God Almighty assigned to a wife is limited to a female, and the position of a husband is limited to a male. Same-sex marriage is just one more attempt by perverted men and women to circumvent the fixed laws of God, and to dishonor His Word.

In a godly and enduring marriage, both the man and the woman recognize their God-given positions as husband and wife. And if God so blesses the union as to grant them children, they each take on another position as father and mother. What husband could be so cruel as to deny his wife as his wife, and what father could be so callous as to deny the mother of his children her God-given title of mother? And what wife and mother can carelessly disregard the positions of her husband as husband and father?

Two of the saddest stories in the Bible are those of Abraham and his son Isaac, both of whom, in a moment of cowardice and unbelief denied their wives, calling them their sisters. The positions of a wife and husband are held in high regard by God who assigned them, and if they are not held in high regard by either the husband or the wife, that neglect or refusal to do so is the equivalent of a slap in the face of God Himself.

Since I have limited myself to 101 pages for this book (which was probably a huge mistake,) I cannot set forth all the duties of a wife in the brief space I now have left, but in reality, there is no need for me to do so, for the duties of a wife are beautifully condensed in a single verse in I Timothy 5:14 –

I will therefore that the younger women marry, bear children, guide the house, give none occasion for the adversary to speak reproachfully.

Within those four duties mentioned in this single verse, the Holy Spirit has given us one duty of a woman before marriage – she is to be married, making her a wife. Secondly, the wife is to bear children, which makes her a mother. These are her two positions. Fulfilling those two positions requires that she – (a) guide the house, and (b) give no occasion for the adversaries of marriage to speak reproachfully against marriage and its sanctity. No man can, without violating God's prescribed order, occupy the position of the wife. He honors his wife's position by occupying, and fulfilling the duties of his own. There may be times when the husband or wife will be called upon to fulfill certain duties within the position of the other, but neither can ever encroach upon, or usurp the position of the other. If the wife is too ill to guide the house, the husband, if he is a husband, will joyfully take hold, and guide the household for as long as is necessary. And the God-given duty of not giving the adversaries of marriage any occasion to speak reproachfully against it is a shared responsibility, enjoined to both the husband and wife.

The wife honors her husband when she (a) **takes his name.** She has left (not abandoned,) her own family name, and has taken the surname of her husband as her own. This is not a light thing. All her life she has been known by the last name of her father. She has answered to that name when called upon. She honored that name every time she put her signature upon a document, check, or contract. And now she is to be called by your name for the rest of her life. Each time she signs a check, a document, or any other written instrument, she is honoring you and your name. And are you not highly honored when she tells her new friends – "We are Mr. and Mrs. Arvil Jones?"

The wife honors her husband when she (b) ***honors his person.*** She is proud to call him her husband. She will do him good and not evil all the days of his life. His heart ***safely trusts*** in her. She honors him in keeping herself for him alone, never being touched by another man. When asked about her husband, she proudly tells her friends who he is, what he is, what he does, and what he stands for. At the age of five, I recall walking hand in hand with my mother along the streets of Detroit Michigan. And out of all the many things I saw and heard, and of all the other things I could have retained in my memory, one thing, more than any other, has stayed with me all these years. I remember passing by a line of men, some very young, and others much older, all standing outside a factory, waiting to go in and fill out an application for a job. As my mother and I passed, every man in that line removed his hat, nodding to my mother, calling her Mrs. Jones, and asking – *"How is Mr. Jones and your family?"* My mother carried herself in such a way that men, all men, honored her. They honored her because she honored her husband, and spoke highly of him.

The wife honors her husband when she (c) ***honors his privacy***. In the same way the husband should never boast to other men about those sacred things that happen between husband and wife, neither should the wife carelessly divulge sacred things to her friends and neighbors. In a marriage where either the husband or wife feel that they must *"share"* the details of their intimacy with others, there is a very serious defect of character, and a serious deficiency of love and honor.

The wife honors her husband when she (d) **renders that godly reverence** and respect which God, in His Word, has enjoined unto her. Wherever she may go, and to whomever she may speak, she speaks highly of her husband. Those who hear her know that her husband is the love of her life, and no other man under heaven can ever take her from him. And finally; **the husband and wife honor each other when** – they honor **that God-given privilege** which He graciously gave to the first man and woman. In honoring one another in every area of the marriage relationship, the husband and wife honor God and His Word. Of what value to God or mankind is a relationship which never displays the honor, the dignity, or the integrity of the One who created life with all its graces? And how can any human relationship display these things if the persons in that relationship do not know their Creator personally? And how can they know Him personally without knowing His Word? And how can they know His Word without a preacher? And how shall they preach, except they be sent?

Before moving on to my last enduring principle – *"**patience**"*, I must return to the verse at the beginning of this book – Hebrews 13:4. I have dealt briefly with the latter part of that verse, but now is the time to go back and deal with the first part – Marriage is honorable in all. Nearly every commentary I have read, and virtually every other minister with whom I have made an acquaintance, have all agreed that the word **"*things*"** should be added to the end of that first clause. They agree that the word **"*things*"**, although not written, is nevertheless **"*implied"*.** And after having consulted a few other *"versions"* of the Bible, I find that many of them have the first part of this verse – "Marriage should be honored by all..." I prefer letting the verse stand as it is in the King James Version:

Marriage is honorable in all, and the bed undefiled: but whoremongers and adulterers God will judge.

If Marriage is honorable in all, why is it that all men, including many ministers, do not honor it? There can be only one reason why men do not honor Marriage, that reason being they do not consider it honorable. And those who do not consider it honorable cannot honor it in any respect, let alone in all respects. It is the man or woman who does not honor Marriage who is quick to dishonor it. These are the men and women who can so easily, without any shame or reservation, commit adultery, fornication, and any other despicable act of sexual perversity. To honor Marriage is to honor every aspect of it, and there is only one Source of information which covers every aspect of Marriage – the Holy Bible. The sanctity of Marriage is not limited to only a few chapters and verses in the Bible. There is not a single Book among the sixty-six Books of the Bible which does not record something about the sanctity of Marriage. Some of those Books, of course, contain more than others on the subject, but all of them, without exception, to some degree, honor that blessed and sacred union.

You are at liberty to disregard, or even contradict any opinion this writer has expressed in this book, but none of us have the liberty to disregard or contradict the clear teaching of the inspired Scriptures. Take my comments for whatever they are worth to you, and do with them what you will, but I beg of you, do not neglect your Holy Bible, if you have one. Here are my closing comments on the meaning of – Marriage is honorable in all: Marriage is not only honorable *in all things* which pertain to marriage, it is also honorable *in all places* on Earth. There is not a continent or an inhabited island upon which Marriage is not honored to some degree. But let us not make the mistake of ascribing the wrong definition to our terms. To say that something is honorable does not necessarily mean that it is honored. The fact that fallen men and women choose to dishonor sacred things does not make them any less honorable. Everything which our Creator and Redeemer made is honorable, and to refuse to honor it is the same as dishonoring it. It is because of the honor which God Himself bestowed upon Marriage that He will judge the whoremonger and the adulterer who dishonors Marriage. Why did God, in His Word, so strongly proclaim His hatred against the sins of whoredom, adultery, fornication, sodomy, and the like? He did so because those who commit these sins violate the sanctity of Marriage, they dishonor Marriage, and in dishonoring Marriage, they dishonor God Himself.

    If the reader has come this far, you have been patient with the writer, and for that I thank you, for patience is indeed a virtue. Patience is also an ***enduring principle*** upon which an ***enduring marriage*** rests. Without patience on the part of all parties concerned, no marriage can survive, much less be a shining example of what God intended for a marriage to be. When I began this project, much of what I wanted to write was already in my heart. The earlier chapters of this book required less time to write than these last two points – honor and patience. I have determined that I will not rush any part of this book, for each part will reflect the content of my own heart and character. More than once I have asked the reader to be patient while I searched my heart for the proper words by which to convey to the reader what I felt in my heart. As I stated in the introduction to this book, my children, grandchildren, and great grandchildren will someday read this book, and it is not likely that I will be here when they do. And so I must be patient, and be certain that the principles of which I have written are principles which I want them to know, believe, follow, and pass on to succeeding generations.

And as I have often directed the reader to the Holy Bible as his or her first and final authority on every point I have made while writing this little book, I now do the same while trying to say something of value about this sacred term – "*patience*". Where else can we find a better example of patience than in the Book inspired by the most patient being who ever lived? Of the many divine attributes of God, revealed and displayed in the person of our Lord Jesus, with the exception of His eternal love, **His patience** shines as brightly as any other. If our eyes were allowed to behold the countless sparkling jewels in His many glorious crowns, the jewel of His patience would soon grasp, and hold our attention. There is no greater or more glorious example of patience than that of our Savior. And if it were possible to make His patience seem more glorious, it would only be by contrasting His infinite patience with our own infinitely poorer facsimile.

And is there any other area of human existence in which patience is more needful than in a Marriage? I dare say that virtually any reader of this book could take up his or her pen at this point, and set forth in grand and graphic terms, the magnitude of the need for patience in marriage. Any man or woman who has been married for any length of time, especially in this modern age, knows the necessity for patience in the largest sense of the term. And even if a couple should be blessed with such a degree of serenity in their marriage that they seldom if ever needed to employ patience with each other, there are yet other persons, and other things with which to contend, all of which demand a high degree of patience.

The sweet exhortation of the beloved Apostle Paul to the church at Thessalonica should be committed to memory by every believer:

Now we exhort you, brethren, warn them that are unruly, comfort the feebleminded, support the weak, **be patient toward all men** (italics mine). See that none render evil for evil unto any man; but ever follow that which is good, both among yourselves, and to all men (I

Thessalonians 5:14, 15 KJV).

If we would all confess the whole truth, most of us would probably agree that we are capable of being *somewhat patient* with some men, women, and children, but how many of us have the grace to show a high degree of patience *with all men*, women, and children? As a Pastor and former school teacher, I have, for many years, seen firsthand the need for long patience, and some folks require more patience than others. Having visited hospitals, nursing homes, asylums, prisons, and detention centers for the mentally challenged, I have gained the utmost respect and admiration for those who work in these facilities on a daily basis. If they did not have patience when they began working there, patience soon became an absolute necessity in order for them to continue working there.

Having spoken with men, women, and children in so many different settings, and under so many different circumstances, my own patience has been stretched to its utmost limit more times than I care to remember. There have been times when, had it not been for the sweet and gracious restraining power of the Holy Spirit within me, those in my presence would never have guessed that I was a minister. I recall the confession of another dear minister, now in Heaven, telling a small congregation of an occasion when he

– "lost his temper". Looking back on the incident, he said – *"You know folks, we really don't **"lose"** our temper, we **"find"** it."* It seems we only **suspect** that we have a temper until our patience has been totally exhausted, and then we discover that we really do have a temper. But let's define our term before proceeding any further.

Patience = 1. Willing to put up with waiting, pain, trouble, etc.; enduring calmly without complaining or losing self-control; 2. With steady effort or long hard work; quietly persevering.

Some folks, mostly men, and a few ladies, have come to me with no other desire than to sit and talk for a while. They just needed someone who was willing to listen – patiently. Some of these conversations stand out more vividly than others. Not all of those whom I have counseled really needed any counseling at all, they just needed a friend who was willing to take the time to hear what was on their hearts. On more than one occasion, I have had the joy of hearing some of these men and women tell me about their dear parents who had passed away. More than a few have said to me – *"Pastor, if it wasn't for the fact that we are all saved by grace through faith, my dear mother would have made it to Heaven on her patience alone."* What a testimony to the patience of a mother! But in testifying to the patience of his mother, he was also confessing that his own behavior often brought out the need for his mother's patience.

How wonderful it is to behold this blessed virtue in others, and how convicting it is to us when we compare their patience to our own, and see the vast gulf that separates the one from the other. The patience of a godly mother should, and often does, instill in us the desire to have the same kind and degree of patience she possessed. And if the longing for that patience yet exists, that, in itself, is the evidence that we do not yet possess it. There are many people I know who seem to have been born with patience, and others who seem as if they never had any, never will have any, and never want to have any. The sad truth is that, patience, like love, being one of those virtues which ought to distinguish us Christians from the rest of the world, seems to be one of the virtues that is most lacking in some of us.

Patience in marriage is often tested, probably more so than any other characteristic except our love for our spouse and children. In fact, to whatever length our patience can be stretched without breaking, it is to that length our marriage will endure, or be an enduring marriage. Patience is a hallmark of an enduring marriage, as the absence of patience is the hallmark of an endured marriage. And how do we measure the length, breadth, height and depth of our patience? May I humbly submit that patience is not measured in distances, it is measured in determination. Patience is not measured in quantity, but in quality. And if it is true that – "the quality of mercy is not strained", may we also affirm that ***the quality of patience*** should never put a strain on our hearts in showing it to others?

Like any other godly virtue, patience shines brightest after we have experienced the absence of it. In the same way we cannot appreciate the light until we have experienced darkness, neither can we appreciate patience until we have first witnessed the opposite, or absence of it. All of this, of course, is vividly displayed by our Lord Jesus in the parable of the two indebted servants In Matthew 18:23-35. One servant owed the king ten thousand talents, but had nothing to pay. He fell on his knees before the king, pleading for patience. The patient and merciful king graciously forgave him of all that debt. This same servant, after being released from an insurmountable debt, finds another servant who owes him a hundred pence. That servant has nothing to pay, and so falls on his knees, pleading for patience, but finds none. He is cast into prison by the impatient and unmerciful knave. Their fellow servants, upon hearing about the unmercifulness of the first servant, go and tell the king of his dastardly deed. The gracious king has him delivered to the tormentors (debt collectors), until the whole debt – ten thousand talents, is paid in full.

If we are not spiritually blind, we cannot fail to see the connection between mercy, forgiveness, and patience. At the low risk of saying something original, may this author submit – ***in every moment of patience, there is a drop of mercy, and in every drop of mercy, there is a moment of patience.*** For every moment in which patience is shown, another drop of mercy is extended. As it is evident from the parable, some folks simply do not appreciate mercy, patience, and forgiveness. And this absence of appreciation for these virtues reveals the absence of the virtue itself. I have said that some folks *seem to have been born with patience,* and some more so than others, but I must emphasize the word "***seem***". I will neither confirm nor deny that patience can be an inherited trait, for that is above my pay grade, which is another way of saying – I don't know. What I do know is that I was not born with it, and I know thousands of other honest folks who will testify that neither were they born with it. If you believe you were born with patience, I envy you, and I applaud you, but I had to learn it, and from all appearances, and according to my wife, and several others, I have not yet learned all I need to know about it.

The enduring principle of patience is an absolute necessity for an enduring marriage, and if you have any doubts about that, just ask my wife. She is another of those wives and mothers who might get to Heaven for her patience alone if it were not for the fact that we are all saved by grace through faith. Her patience is just one more of the many evidences of the grace that saved her soul forty years ago. I am constantly aware of the grace and patience of my dear wife, for when the subject of patience comes up in a conversation between her and her friends, she tells them how patient her husband is. She never boasts of how patient she has been with me and our three children, but instead boasts of the patience of her husband toward her. She says I am the patient one, I say she is the most patient one.

I cannot overemphasize that patience in a marriage is not optional, but mandatory. It will make the difference between an enduring marriage and an endured marriage. If we go back to those blessed and sacred vows that are so often repeated in a wedding ceremony – we vow to love, honor, cherish, and be faithful – *in sickness and in health.* It is not as difficult to be patient with a person when they are healthy as it is when they are sick. Their sickness may be such that it demands nearly all of our time and attention, taking us away from our television, radio, telephone, I-phone, I-pad, fishing, and golf. It is so easy to take a wife, child, or husband for granted when all is well, but when an illness strikes which may adversely affect our routine, or the whole family, or even the careers of either or both parents, patience can be sorely tested to its limit. When I was ten years old, there were ten children in our little home. In the winter of 1967, the whole family, including Mom and Dad caught the flu. Sick as she was, my mother tended to every child and my father till all of us were well. When I was sixty-one years old, and diagnosed as having had "*numerous*" heart attacks, then undergoing quadruple bypass surgery, unable to work for three months, and unable to do all the things I was used to doing, whatever I could not do for myself, my wife did for me. And she did all this in addition to the usual daily chores she was accustomed to doing. But, as I have often said to many of my friends – the fact that my wife has been at my side for forty-nine years and counting says all that needs to be said about her patience. And those who have known me for any length of time reply – "Amen brother."

In our vows, we promise to love, honor, cherish, and be faithful – ***for richer or for poorer***. It is a good thing my wife didn't marry me for my money, because if she had, she would have been terribly disappointed. God has been so good to us in forty-nine years of marriage, and I am definitely the one who got the better part of the deal in convincing Carolyn to marry me. There have been some lean times in our marriage, but not once have I ever heard her complain about the things we did not have. She was always thankful for the things we did have. She has been patient in the leaner times as well as in the more favorable times. Trust me when I say that my files are full of cases in which the wife told me from her own mouth that she was leaving her husband because he didn't make enough money to support the kind of lifestyle of which she thought she was worthy. Others have confided to me that they were not willing to give up the lifestyle which their husbands had once been able to afford, but could no longer afford due to circumstance beyond his control. And some of the saddest of all cases were those women who left their husbands every time the stock market fell, and returned when the stock went up again. How soon some folks forget what they vowed to do at the ceremony!

In our vows, we promise to love, honor, cherish, and be faithful – ***for better or for worse***. There is no question - my wife got the worst end of the deal when she married me. In the first five years of our marriage, I made her life a living hell with my drinking and carousing. But through it all, she showed a patience of which Job himself would have been envious. And after we were both saved, and I was called to the ministry, her patience never wavered. She was patient when I worked a full time job, pastored a church, and taught school while studying to earn my doctorate. She has been patient when I had to leave her in the wee hours of the morning to go and sit by the bedside of a dying man or woman. She was patient when I was called upon to go to the mission field half a world away. She was patient when we had to give up our vacations because I was called to preach in revival meetings. She has been patient when others spoke evil of her husband, although it was breaking her heart, and she secretly cried in my absence. In her own sickness and pain she has encouraged me to leave her alone at home to go and minister to someone in need.

In our vows, we promise to love, honor, cherish, and be faithful – *for as long as we both shall live*. That is patience. And as admirable as a lifelong patience is, we must never forget that it is, at its best, patience on the human level. And no matter how well our human patience resembles and exemplifies the patience of our Lord, it can never rise to that divine level. If in all things He must have the preeminence, He must have it in this also, for there is no patience that can match His own. His patience, like His Holy Spirit, can be imitated, but never duplicated. And yet I think we do Him a great injustice when we speak only of the patience He showed while in His flesh. Yea, let us go back to the dateless past, when there was yet no man, and no earth for a man to inhabit, before there was a star or a galaxy of countless billions of stars. There is an incalculable date, withheld from mortals, in which countless myriads of angels were created by Him, and for His glory. One of them was Lucifer.

    The Holy Spirit chose to tell us mortals of the rebellion and expulsion of Lucifer and an undisclosed number of angels who rebelled with him, against God and His authority. The inspired writers of Scripture tell us something of the glory, the attributes, and the duties of these mighty and glorious beings. The period between the creation of these beings and their rebellion is a mystery no mortal can know. But if you know the same God that I know, can you imagine Him expelling the rebels the moment their iniquity was made known? Did God slay Adam the moment he sinned against Him? Did God send you and me to Hell the moment we first sinned against Him? Does His infinite patience extend to mortals only, or was he patient with the angels also. Are they not wiser and stronger than us? Are they not more glorious than us? Why, then, should He not bear as long or longer with them, as He has borne with us?

    If I must stand alone in my estimation of the quantity

and quality of His patience, so be it. I reserve the right to be wrong, and I welcome the opportunity of being shown that I am wrong, as long as the one who shows me I am wrong can base his argument upon the everlasting Word of God. Eternity cannot be reckoned and measured as time is reckoned and measured, therefore we can never know how long our God bore with the angels that sinned before He finally cast them down to Hell, for that happened before time, as we know it, was created. But as the renowned nineteenth century preacher and songwriter, Charles Tindley wrote – "We'll understand it better by and by."

And this patient, merciful, gracious and longsuffering God who created all that is, who gave His only begotten Son, that whosoever believeth in Him should not perish, but have everlasting life, is the God who, for no other reason than His own Sovereign will, ordained that sacred union of two persons – a man and a woman, calling it Marriage. How, then, shall we mere mortals dare to ascribe less honor to Marriage than that which its Creator demands in His Word?

In eastern culture, in the days of Christ, it was customary for the man and woman who were betrothed (engaged) to each other to treat the relationship as if she were already his bride, but without coming together (sexually), expecting a ceremony, the feast which accompanied it, and the consummation of the marriage. A wedding of that day was accompanied by great pomp and circumstance, singing and dancing, with the ten bridesmaids rejoicing with and for the bride to be. In this age of grace, Christ is not yet wedded to His bride, but treats the relationship as if He were. The wedding itself, of course, will take place in the heavenlies. In the space I have left, may I extend to you an urgent and gracious invitation to prepare yourself now to go to that greatest of all gatherings, for if you arrive without the wedding garment bearing the insignia of the Groom Himself, you will surely be cast into outer darkness forever.

If any dear soul has endured my coarse manners this far, I thank you from the depths of my heart, and say – God bless you till we meet again.

In closing, I am humbled and yet unafraid to say with the patriarch Job – Also now, behold, my witness is in heaven, and my record is on high (Job 16:19 KJV).

www.ingramcontent.com/pod-product-compliance
Lightning Source LLC
Chambersburg PA
CBHW061641040426
42446CB00010B/1528